POLITICAL ORDER

POLITICAL ORDER

PHILOSOPHICAL ANTHROPOLOGY, MODERNITY, AND THE CHALLENGE OF IDEOLOGY

David J. Levy

Louisiana State University Press
Baton Rouge and London

Designer: Diane Batten Didier
Typeface: Linotron Trump
Typesetter: G&S Typesetters, Inc.
Printer: Thomson-Shore, Inc.
Binder: John H. Dekker & Sons

10 9 8 7 6 5 4 3 2 1

Library of Congress Cataloging in Publication Data
Levy, David J.
  Political order.

  Includes index.
  1. Political obligation.   2. Political obligation—
Philosophy.   3. Ideology.   4. Technology and civiliza-
tion.   5. Philosophical anthropology.   I. Title.
JC329.5.L48   1987   320'.01'1   87-13546
ISBN 0-8071-1389-1

CONTENTS

PREFACE

   Political Order is, as its title suggests, an inquiry into the fundamental features of a form of existence characteristic of the human species as such. In a previous work, *Realism: An Essay in Interpretation and Social Reality* (Manchester, 1981), I began by posing the question, What is Social Reality? answering it in the title of the book's final chapter "Political Existence." The present work is an attempt to explicate the anthropological and ontological assumptions already present in that answer.

   My inquiry falls into three sections. The first, consisting of chapters 1 to 3, draws primarily on the work of philosophical anthropologists influenced by the seminal work of Max Scheler and on the ontology of Nicolai Hartmann, which provides their conception of man's nature and place in the cosmos with an appropriate metaphysical basis. In this first section, I shall be concerned above all with understanding political activity as a special requirement of a being possessing a certain scientifically identifiable biophysical constitution, a "human nature," and occupying a particular place in the order of things, "nature." In chapters 4 to 6, I shall examine the limitations of this approach and, through discussion of the work of Eric Voegelin, suggest ways in which the deficiencies can be remedied by a philosophy of consciousness and history such as he developed. Thus, while taking account of the findings of a biophysically oriented anthropology, I shall set these in the context of a broader and deeper understanding of human consciousness and of the process of reality that is registered in man's psyche. If the first three chapters help the reader to understand the necessity of politics as a specifically human activity, chapters 4 to 6 are intended to illuminate the question of political order, conceived as the result of man's efforts to attune himself to the order of Being in which he knows himself to be a participant and of which, ontologically speaking, nature and human nature are merely fragments.

The juxtaposition of Voegelin's work to that of the post-Schelerian anthropologists is not motivated by the deceptive hope of achieving a synthesis between what, as I learned above all from Gregor Sebba, are very different approaches to the question of man and his place in reality. At best we may find that there is a certain fruitful complementarity between the two; a complementarity that may help us in the final section of the book, where the insights of both will be utilized in an attempt to understand the problem of political order as it arises in the typical conditions of modernity.

While the intellectual value of my juxtaposition of the two approaches can only be judged in terms of any success I may have in deepening the reader's understanding of man's political existence, there is some historical justification for the form of my enterprise in the fact that Voegelin's work, as well as that of those I shall call the philosophical anthropologists, takes its cue from certain themes announced in the late work of Scheler. Like the philosophical anthropologists, Voegelin found in Scheler's philosophy a point of departure for his effort to comprehend the disorder of his times. Although the paths are different, both examine aspects of matters that are, as Scheler himself insisted, necessary to the attainment of human self-understanding. If one accepts, as I do, Scheler's judgment on this point, it follows that whatever may be the value of any conclusions that emerge from the present inquiry, the area of questions that it explores is that in which any possible answers to the problem of political order will have to be found.

ACKNOWLEDGMENTS

I am grateful to the editor and publishers of the *Journal of the British Society for Phenomenology* for permission to republish the substance of my paper "Politics, Nature and Freedom: On the Natural Foundation of the Political Condition" as chapter 3 of the present work, and to the editors and publishers of the *Journal of the Anthropological Society of Oxford* to republish part of "The Anthropological Horizon: Max Scheler, Arnold Gehlen and the Idea of a Philosophical Anthropology," which first appeared in its pages and now forms part of chapter 4.

Above all I wish to acknowledge my debt of gratitude to the late Professor Gregor Sebba, whose encouragement and advice enabled me to recast an earlier and much cruder version of this book in its present form. It is to his memory and that of Professor Eric Voegelin that I wish to dedicate this work in the hope that, for all its faults, this essay may be acknowledged as a contribution to the clarification of the problem and mystery of human political order.

Political Order

ONE

NATURE AND HUMAN NATURE

Politics is a human activity, one of those aspects of human existence which, because it is apparently unique to our species, has been regarded as definitive of man's nature. There are many varieties of social animal in the world, but man, it can be argued, stands alone as a political animal; for in his case, to a unique extent, the form of social life enjoyed or endured depends upon decision and deliberation rather than on the unreasoning imperatives of instinct. There are other, complementary ways of putting it. Man can be described as free because his position in the world is such that his destiny in life depends upon decisions that he makes. He can be called rational because these decisions are made in a self-conscious way in the light of his understanding of himself and his condition. He may be termed a creature of culture because the reality of his life depends enormously on what he makes of himself and how he conceives his nature. Political man, free man, rational or cultural man are alternative labels but do not designate opposed concepts of human nature.

Politics as a field of theoretical inquiry is a study of the possibilities of human existence—what men have realized in the past and what they may hope to do in the future. Since all human activity is the activity of individuals of a given species taking place in the context of a given but not unchanging environment, an attempt to grasp what these possibilities may be requires that, in the first place, we should try to identify the specific nature of man and of the structure of the world that forms the limiting context of his action.

But there is at once a problem—the problem of "human nature." For *human nature* is an essentially contested term. It is not merely that there are many competing concepts of what human nature is, but that some have argued that "human nature" is a part of our intellectual heritage that we could well do without. In so far as its use suggests that there is a fixed repertoire of possibilities inherent in the species, it belongs to a world-view that we have now outgrown. When people believed that each species was created completed and unchanging according to its kind by God, it made sense to talk about "human nature" and even to derive the character of political society from its supposed features. But now we know that ours is not a world of static forms. The theory of evolution tells us that species develop through the interaction of the organism with its environment, and that the balance of features within a population alters depending upon its worldly context. In the case of man, moreover, that context is increasingly the product of his own world-transforming activity. If men make and remake themselves without ceasing, then at best the reality of a universal human archetype belongs as much to our past as the Platonic ontology that enshrined it as model and explanation alike. At worst, *human nature* remains a term not of science but of ideology—a phrase that men use to legitimate institutions and practices that preserve the privileges of a given class, race, or sex at the expense of the rest of mankind.

At first sight even modern ontology—often considered the last refuge of a near-extinct essentialism—leaves no room for the venerable concept of a fixed and finite human nature. As Nicolai Hartmann puts it:

> In the real world we are confronted with no rigid system, not even with a world "finished" in every respect, which is simply taken as a fact and in which there remains nothing for us to do. It is an old error to think that being is the opposite of motion and becoming. . . . Becoming is no opposite of being but is a form of being. Everything real is in flux, involved in a constant coming into, or going out of, existence. Motion and becoming form the universal mode of being of the real, no matter whether it be a question of material things,

living forms, or human beings. Rest and rigidity are only found in
the ideal essences of the old ontology.[1]

In our post-Darwinian age the ghost of Heraclitus would seem finally to have triumphed over Parmenides and his influential identification of the ultimately real with the absolutely changeless. Yet
matters are not so simple, as is obvious when we consider that
today the stoutest defenders of the explanatory value of the concept of human nature are to be found among thinkers like the
ethologist Konrad Lorenz and Edward O. Wilson, the founder of
sociobiology, whose work is firmly based in the Darwinian theory
of evolution.

The oddity of this situation is somewhat lessened when we
remember, with Raymond Williams, that *nature* is "perhaps the
most complex word in the language." Williams distinguishes three
areas of meaning: "(i) the essential quality and character *of* something; (ii) the inherent force which directs either the world or human beings or both; (iii) the material world itself, taken as including or not including human beings."[2] The same author sometimes
slips from one use to the other, and the reader is hardly aware of
what has happened.

To deploy the terms *nature* and *human nature* alongside each
other is to draw, more or less consciously, on the rich ambiguity of
the word. Clarity in argument is a virtue, and since it is scarcely
encouraged by the use of ambiguous terms their conscious deploy-
ment requires justification. A prime aim of this chapter is therefore
to justify its admittedly ambiguous title. It stands at the beginning
of an inquiry into the foundations of political order because, it
seems to me, human nature in the first sense of essential character
is bound to play a central part in my argument, and because nature
in the third sense of "material world"—an overnarrow definition
of reality, as will emerge—must be accepted as the presumptive
foundation of everything that happens in the world. On Williams'
second sense—the inherent force that directs either the world or
human beings or both—I prefer to be less explicit. If such a force
can be identified it can only be known, rather than accepted as an

1. Nicolai Hartmann, *New Ways of Ontology*, trans. Reinhard C. Kuhn (Chicago,
1952), 28–29.
2. Raymond Williams, *Keywords: A Vocabulary of Culture and Society* (London,
1976), 184.

act of faith, by examination of nature in the other two senses. Perhaps we cannot avoid speaking of it—perhaps we *should* not—but we would do well to approach it with considerable caution. If it is the field of ultimate truth, it is no less the domain of integral illusion.

The question of the relationship between nature and human nature is at first glance a question about the way in which a particular species is related to its environment. That this relationship should be questionable by one of its elements is, indeed, one of its peculiar features. Man is a living being and, as with all living beings, his life is sustained by what he draws from his environment. If we are to say what, if anything, is unique about man's particular mode of existence, it will be helpful to distinguish the various forms of dependence upon environment that characterize different types of living being. Such an examination cannot be exhaustive. Every species of plant and animal has its own special relationship to its surroundings. It survives only because it is a specialist in its particular field, although the degree of specialization and therefore adaptability varies widely. But, as Max Scheler showed, a typology of living forms need not be exhaustive in order to be illuminating.[3] The distinctions we habitually draw between plant and animal, animal and man are, for some purposes, scientifically unsatisfactory. The real borderlines are not so clear-cut. Even the apparently absolute boundary between the living and the inert is transgressed by viruses. The distinctions of common sense are, nevertheless, a good starting point for inquiry, corresponding as they do to the broad divisions within the realm of life.

Scheler believed that:

> The limits of psychic life coincide with the boundaries of organic life itself. . . . The lowest form of psychic life is a vital feeling, drive or impulse devoid of consciousness, sensation and representation. It is the power behind every activity, even behind those on the highest spiritual level, and it provides the energy for the purest acts of thought and the most tender expressions of good will. As the terms imply, "feeling" and "impulse" are not yet separated. Impulse always has a specific direction, a goal-orientation "toward something," for example, nourishment or sexual satisfaction. A bare movement "to-

3. Max Scheler, *Man's Place in Nature*, trans. Hans Meyerhoff (Boston, 1961).

ward," as toward light, or "away from," as a state of pleasure or suf-
fering devoid of object, are the only two modes of this primitive feeling. Yet this impulse is quite different from the centers and fields of
energy that we associate with the image of inorganic bodies without
consciousness. . . . The vital feeling of the plant is directed toward
its medium, toward the growing into this medium in accordance
with certain directions like "above" and "below," toward the light or
toward the earth, but only toward the undifferentiated whole of these
directions. It reacts to possible resistances and realities along these
general lines which are important for the life of the organism, but
not to specific constituents and stimuli in the environment to which
particular sensory qualities or primitive representatives would correspond. The plant, for example, reacts specifically to the intensity
of the light rays but not to particular colors and the directions of
these rays.[4]

Animal life displays a more active and differentiated orientation
toward its environment. Here we encounter, first, the phenomenon
of instinctive behavior. Recognizing the difficulty of defining instinct in psychological terms, Scheler begins by offering a definition in terms of behavior. He distinguishes five features of instinctive behavior. First, it must be meaningful in the objective sense of
serving the life chances of the living organism primarily through
the contribution that it makes to nourishment and reproduction.
Second, it must show a definitive unchanging rhythm. Instinctive
behavior is not reducible to the mechanistic pattern of stimulus/
response, for it is activated in conditions that the individual animal
has not previously experienced and even in the absence of any
models that it might imitate. Consequently, the purpose of instinctive behavior can refer to situations—future contingencies—that
are not part of the animal's immediate environment in time and
space. The squirrel prepares for winter in advance and the swallow
for the eggs yet to be laid. Third, instinctive behavior provides
appropriate responses only for typically recurrent situations in the
life of the species, not for the particular experiences of the individual. Fourth, instinct is innate and hereditary in the species. This
does not mean that the young animal is capable of immediate utilization of the full range of its instinctual equipment. The possibility

4. *Ibid.*, 8–9.

of actualizing certain innate behavioral patterns may be coordi-
nated with fixed stages of individual maturation. Sexually orien-
tated behavior is overwhelmingly of this type. Finally, instinctive
behavior is complete—a patterned whole—from the start. It is
not learned in a succession of attempts to deal with a problem as a
gradual accumulation of movements that have proved successful.

Beyond instinct, animal behavior involves associative memory,
intelligence, and choice. By "associative memory" Scheler means
the capacity to learn from individual experience on a trial-and-
error basis. While this is a very widespread feature of animal life,
the next level of psychic activity—intelligence—is a much rarer
phenomenon. Scheler offers a behavioral and a psychological definition of intelligence. An organism may be said to behave intelli-
gently when it satisfies the following conditions:

> It must be capable of responding, without trial and error, to a new
> situation meaningfully, "cleverly" or "foolishly"; that is, aiming at a
> goal but missing it, for only one who is intelligent can be foolish.
> It must be capable of solving the drive-determined problem sud-
> denly and, above all, independently of the number of previous at-
> tempts. . . . On the psychological side, we can define intelligence as
> a sudden insight into a connected context of facts and values within
> the environment that is not perceived directly now or ever was per-
> ceived previously so that it is a function of reproduction. . . . Intelli-
> gence is insight into a state of affairs on the basis of a structure of
> relations whose basic elements are partly given in experience, partly
> completed in anticipatory representation. . . . Anticipation . . . is al-
> ways characteristic of this type of thinking which is productive, not
> reproductive. It is a kind of prevision of a new state of affairs never
> experienced before. . . . The difference between intelligence and as-
> sociative memory is obvious: the situation to be grasped and to be
> mastered is not only new and atypical for the species, but above
> all new for the individual. Such an objectively meaningful behavior
> takes place suddenly and prior to new trials, and independent of the
> number of previous trials.[5]

In attributing intelligence in this sense to certain animals,
Scheler relied considerably on the experiments carried out by

5. *Ibid.*, 29–30.

Wolfgang Köhler at his research station on Tenerife. Köhler's findings, published in 1925, are a classic in their field, for he showed that the problem-solving actions of chimpanzees involve something more than a trial-and-error approach. The chimpanzee, like the other great apes, is capable of grasping a situation as a whole and planning for it with a considerable degree of abstraction. Puzzlement, which Scheler considers as originating in the frustration of particular vital drives, provokes mental exertion as the animal strives to grasp the dimensions of his problem and discover the suitable solution. While the process is underway, the animal may hardly move, and when a possible solution occurs to him the experience is reflected in his facial expression. Köhler called this an "Aha!" experience. The degree of relatively abstract thought involved is suggested by the sequence puzzlement-consideration-insight, which is evident from the ape's behavior. Of course this reading of the evidence has been challenged. There are, after all, those who deny our right to retain such mentalistic terms as *consideration* and *insight*, even in the psychological study of man. While I cannot deal with such objections here, the reader may be referred to Mary Midgley's excellent discussion of this and related issues in *Beast and Man.*[6] Midgley shows not only that the behaviorist account of the reactions of higher animals is inadequate but that no illegitimate anthropomorphism is involved in applying to related animals the terms we find indispensable in the analysis of our own motives and actions.

The complexity of the animal's relationship to its environment, especially where intelligence in Scheler's sense is involved, means that the animal must be capable of choice. This is so even though, as Scheler stresses, the roots of motivation in man as well as animal are sunk in the subsoil of preconscious "drives."

The animal is not a mechanism of instinct, associations and conditioned reflexes. In the first place, the system of drives is highly differentiated: it consists of dominant drives, and executive, subordinate and auxiliary drives; again, of drives concerned with the performance of general and specific tasks. In the second place, the animal has a drive center corresponding to the unified structure of its nervous system. It is capable of intervening spontaneously in its

6. Mary Midgley, *Beast and Man: The Roots of Human Nature* (London, 1979).

constellation of drives from this central organization so that, to a
certain extent at least, it can avoid immediate gratifications in order
to obtain greater gratifications that are more distant in time and may
involve a circuitous route.[7]

To speak of choice is to speak of freedom, and if Scheler's analysis is accepted we must allow that the higher animal is endowed
with a degree of free will. In the case of man, the space of freedom
is greatly increased because man's relationship to his cosmic context is fundamentally different. The intelligence of the animal is
exclusively practical intelligence, always directed toward the satisfaction of a sensed need. The interaction between animal and environment is such that each is stabilized in its place. Human action, in contrast, opens up the world. Scheler attributes this to the
fact that man is not only a conscious but a spiritual being, and he
defines a spiritual being as one able to say *no* to its immediate
environment. Spirit, in this sense, is the source not only of asceti-
cism but of every project directed at altering man's surrounding
field. Human self-consciousness and the ability to objectify his
environment, as well as his own physiological and psychological
states, combine with a capacity to discover causal connections
within and between these elements to make man a "world-open"
being. His nature is not infinitely plastic, nor is nature as he encounters it in his environment. Reality subsists prior to being explored or explained and can be recognized as such by its resistance
to consciousness. The real shark is the one that cannot be thought
out of the swimmer's experience.

Man's relationship to his environment is not static. In acting
in the world man does not so much transform himself, as some
have thought, as seek to realize possibilities and values that only
a spiritual being with a capacity to negate the immediately given
could envisage. He opens up the immediate environment to make
it his world. The real world is such that certain conceivable
possibilities, but not all, can be realized. And this also is not a
static position, for there are times and places where certain ontological possibilities are more or less available. Every historical subject, group, or civilization has its own range of possibilities—a fi-

7. Scheler, *Man's Place in Nature,* 33–34.

nite province within the greater but still finite world of mankind. Max Scheler's work has exerted a considerable influence on the development of philosophical anthropology, especially in Germany, in the half century or so since its publication. There are, it is true, considerable problems in Scheler's identification of the limits of psychic with those of organic life. It is not merely counter-intuitive to attribute psychic life to plants; it suggests a tendency to extend the meaning of a category to the point where it ceases to be analytically useful. This, in turn, is connected with the fact that, when Scheler wrote this book close to the end of his life, his ideas on the relationship of nature and human nature had become bound up with a pantheist or at least panpsychic outlook that envisaged the process of reality as the gradual realization of spirit in the world. He looked back to Hegel and Spinoza for the ancestry of his view that "the basic relationship between man and the Ground of Being consists in the fact that this Ground comprehends and realizes itself directly in man, who, both as spirit and as life, is but a partial mode of the eternal spirit and drive."[8]

In such passages as this, Scheler is extending the line of his inquiry into areas that will concern us in later chapters. There we will have cause to question the adequacy of the terms in which Scheler articulates his awareness of the irreducibility of the process of reality to the facts of nature, even while allowing that it is precisely the failure of some of his successors to guard against such a reduction that limits the value of their achievement. Superior to Scheler in the precision with which they examine man's biophysical nature and condition, they fail to grasp the measure of the problem of transcendence that loomed so large in his thought and finds more adequate articulation in the work of Voegelin. However, such issues can wait, for nothing we can learn from their examination will invalidate Scheler's fundamental argument thus far—that man is rooted in nature and that even in transcending it he retains within himself the forces that decisively determine life at its lower levels. We are so accustomed to think in terms of contrasts between culture and nature, heredity and environment, spirit and body, cause and purpose, instinct and free will, that it is something of a

8. *Ibid.*, 92.

salutory shock to encounter a thinker who suggests a way in which
all these categories—each born, after all, from our efforts to understand ourselves—can be integrated in a coherent theory of man.
The need for such a theory is inherent in the very human condition that it aims to clarify. The project of a philosophical anthropology is implied in certain defining features of human existence.
Because man is relatively free from the constraints of his immediate environment the range of options open to him is unparalleled
in the rest of creation. Because he can objectify the elements and
forces that surround him, and can picture himself as one actor
among others in the general drama, he is bound to develop a more
or less coherent view of the world within which his life appears as
a significant item. Man endows the world with meaning, though
whether this meaning corresponds to an ultimate universal order
or purpose must forever remain a mystery. From the place of man,
which is within the putative order, total knowledge, which would
be knowledge of the totality, is not to be had.

There are two ways of conceiving this situation, which for convenience I shall call the Kantian and the Platonic. The Kantian,
influenced by criteria of evidence drawn from the sciences of nature, accepts that the mystery is impenetrable and draws the conclusion that the meaning of things is always and exclusively a human attribution, though one perhaps conditioned and provoked by
what is not human in origin. Thus Hartmann writes: "The opposite of what the metaphysicians have always thought is true: precisely a meaningless world is the only meaningful world for a being
like man: in a world full of meaning even without him, he with his
gifts of bestowing meaning would be superfluous."[9] The Platonist,
while accepting also the mystery that is inseparable from the fact
of human finitude—the mystery of ultimate origins and destiny—
accepts too the validity of psychic experience whose evidence may
be subjectively compelling but which is untestable by reference to
the facts of the external world. So Voegelin, using the terminology
as well as the themes of Plato, writes: "Man experiences himself
as tending beyond his human imperfection toward the perfection
of the divine ground that moves him." And again:

9. Nicolai Hartmann, *Aesthetik* (Berlin, 1953), cited by Herbert Spiegelberg in
The Phenomenological Movement: A Historical Introduction (2 vols.; The Hague,
1960), I, 408.

... existence is not a fact. If anything existence is the non-fact of a disturbing movement in the In-Between of ignorance and knowledge, of time and timelessness, of imperfection and perfection, of hope and fulfillment, and ultimately of life and death. From the experience of this movement, from the anxiety of losing the right direction in this In-Between of darkness and light, arises the enquiry concerning the meaning of life. But it does arise . . . because life is experienced as man's participation in a movement with a direction to be found or missed; if man's existence were not a movement but a fact, it would not only have no meaning but the question of meaning could not even arise.[10]

One should not make the mistake of identifying the Kantian and Platonic perspectives with nonreligious and religious outlooks respectively. The Kantian view is quite compatible with a religious belief based upon acceptance of special revelation, whereas, as the example of Plato himself makes clear, the Platonic conception of the relationship between existence and meaning does not depend upon the experience of a personal epiphany. Both are properly philosophical positions that depend upon conscious experience refined by reflection on the significance of what is naturally disclosed in life. The terms *refinement* and *reflection* refer to the fact that neither is an immediate intuition of the truth of reality and that both are reached by the rational investigation of experience itself and the no less rational criticism of other, less differentiated ways of expressing the structure of existence. They are both hermeneutic at two levels. Each offers an interpretation of existence that is in part reached by critical interpretation of other terms in which human existence can, more primitively, be expressed.[11]

It is worth pausing here to consider certain aspects of the prephilosophical world-views that precede and underlie the sophisticated Kantian and Platonic anthropologies. In the present context they are of interest for three reasons. First, by their content, which is anthropological and ontological, they may throw some direct light on the relationship between man and the world he inevitably

10. Eric Voegelin, *Anamnesis*, trans. Gerhart Niemeyer (Notre Dame, Ind., 1978), 103; Eric Voegelin, "The Gospel and Culture," in D. Miller and D. G. Hadidian (eds.) *Jesus and Man's Hope* (2 vols; Pittsburgh, 1971), II, 63.

11. David J. Levy, *Realism: An Essay in Interpretation and Social Reality* (Manchester, 1981), 46–57.

inhabits. Second, by their form, which is mythical, they may clarify some of the problems we face in trying to determine the relationship between meaning and existence. Third, by their lack of conceptual differentiation they may illustrate a perennial temptation of human thought, which Hartmann calls the prejudice in favor of simplicity—a prejudice whose effects are not confined to the world of archaic myth but manifest themselves wherever we attempt to interpret the complex structure of human existence in terms of categories derived from only one of its component levels, whether it be material, inorganic or organic nature, consciousness, or spirit. Odd though it sounds, this means that the character of archaic myth, expressed in religious symbolism, gives us a clue to understanding the mistake involved in modern reductionist theories that explain man's nature and condition as being merely the complex effect of mechanical or biological causes. I have in mind not only the behaviorism of B. F. Skinner but also the popular understanding of sociobiology that holds that "the qualities we value as most human—altruism, morality, religion, even love— are merely the survival strategies of our 'selfish' genes, biologically evolved through millions of years before we were human . . . and still operating today."[12]

In approaching these issues I shall be guided by Mircea Eliade's treatment of religious symbolism and myth. Referring to the author of *The Golden Bough*, Eliade writes: "Where a Frazer could see nothing but 'superstition,' a metaphysic was already implicit, even though it was expressed by a pattern of symbols rather than by the interplay of concepts: a metaphysic—that is, a whole and coherent conception of Reality, not a series of instinctive gestures ruled by the same fundamental 'reaction of the human animal in confrontation with Nature.'"[13]

Eliade calls the implicit metaphysic of religious symbolism "archaic ontology." This is, in one sense, a misleading phrase, for the conception of reality intended is not confined to the religious universe of archaic or nonliterate peoples. In Eliade's view, it is the living core of the religious view of the world as such. When the

---

12. These words come from the cover of the Bantam paperback of Edward O. Wilson, *On Human Nature* (New York, 1979).

13. Mircea Eliade, *Images and Symbols: Studies in Religious Symbolism*, trans. Philip Mairet (London, 1961), 176.

intelligible essence of myth, rite, and symbol is grasped we find not a shoddy tissue of transparent superstition conditioned by every-day fears but a creative interpretation of human existence as participation in universal, living, cosmological order. The fundamental psychic problem that man faces is how he may interpret his existence as meaningful in spite of the disasters that befall him. Somehow the order that the psyche desires must be matched to the experienced nature of the cosmos. As Eliade puts it, the terror of history must be overcome, for history tears the fabric of meaning by bringing everything to oblivion.

There are, it seems to me, two elements in the terror of history that we must distinguish if we are to understand fully the genius of archaic ontology. Certainly it is partly a matter of mundane fear—the encroaching hostilities of war or the spreading plague—but partly it is something else, the *angst* or anxiety of which Heidegger speaks. Anxiety is unlike fear in having no definite object. It is rooted in man's awareness of the limit of his life in time, a feature of conscious finitude. Fear is particular and individual, anxiety is universal. Yet while fear, being conditioned or spontaneous, can break into life at any moment, anxiety—a constitutive element of human life—can be rendered impotent by a sufficiently powerful system of belief. It is easier to imagine a civilization where everyone faced thè prospect of his own death with an easy mind than one in which no one was frightened by spiders.

In so far as there is a historical dimension to archaic ontology it is a "sacred history," which, in the form of myth, recounts the origins of the cosmos or any part of it. It tells how the earth was made as it is by the gods and of the exemplary deeds of heroes. Through myth, man accounts for his own existence and nature as well as that of the cosmos. Myths tell him what he is and why. They "preserve and transmit the paradigms, the exemplary models, for all responsible activities in which men engage. By virtue of these paradigmatic models revealed to men in mythical times, the Cosmos and society are periodically regenerated."[14] Myth recounts events that happened in the time of origins, *in illo tempore*—the "once-upon-a-time" when everything was new—and this mythical time can be reactualized through the ritual repetition of archetypal ges-

14. Mircea Eliade, *The Myth of the Eternal Return,* trans. Willard R. Trask (Princeton, 1954), xiv.

tures and events. To recollect or repeat is to reactualize a time when everything was uncorrupted, to participate in the renewal of the original act of creation by which the ordered cosmos was brought out of chaos.

Stated like this, the idea of regeneration of the world is difficult for the modern Westerner to grasp. The image of the arrow of time, expressing the irreversibility of the historical moment, is deeply ingrained in our consciousness. Yet the regenerative urge survives in more or less covert form. When the flight of time's arrow is conceived as a rational or at least intelligible process, the result is the sort of historicist philosophy which, in its utopian aspect, makes its own all the regenerative dreams of primal and now ultimate innocence. What was once thought to belong exclusively to the origins is attributed to the destination of man's world. In the theology of Jürgen Moltmann and the philosophy of Ernst Bloch this is a fully conscious appropriation. Elsewhere it is not, but the magnetic power of the dream of regeneration survives every metamorphosis. Nor is it impossible to understand the significance that the repetition of archetypal gestures and events has for archaic man. Our own ceremonies and celebrations recall culturally and spiritually significant events, and in at least one case—the celebration of Holy Communion—what is involved is nothing less than the reactualization of an event which, in terms of historical time, belongs to the past. The sacred time of the Mass and the presence of Christ's sacrifice within it testify to a continuity between Christianity and the most profound conception of archaic ontology.

The universality of archaic ontology is rooted in the unity of mankind as a symbol-making animal and the endurance of the fundamental ontological conditions to which he responds. From the conjunction of the two—the creative interplay of psyche and cosmos—is born a coherent interpretation of existence which, to a unique extent, provides man with answers to the questions that trouble him most deeply. The symbols of religion reveal a continuity between the structures of human existence and those of the cosmos. They allow man to banish the haunting sense of isolation in a cold and heartless universe—to see himself as a partner in a world of order. When archaic man interprets his life by analogy with the repetitive and cyclical rhythms of nature, he lays claim to a unity between psychic and cosmic reality that soothes the fear of

oblivion. Never far from death, he knows that when the moon vanishes from the sky the darkness is only a prelude to its return. The
barren surface of the winter landscape is no more than a screen
before the promise of spring renewal. As part of the cosmos, archaic
man sees his life as subject to the same reassuring rhythms. No
end is final, and no merely historical disaster is more than a moment in a process that renews and restores. "The religious symbols
which point to the structures of life . . . unveil the miraculous, inexplicable side of life, and at the same time the sacramental dimension of human existence. 'Deciphered' in the light of religious symbols, human life reveals a hidden side: it comes from 'another part,'
from far off; it is 'divine' in the sense that it is the work of the gods
or of supernatural beings."[15] Thus religious symbols not only bind
the structures of psyche and cosmos in a tight web of meaning but
also serve to link the limited space of experienced reality with
the mysterious unknown out of which it emerges and into which
it passes. What happened *in illo tempore* provides the mind with
sufficient reason for the world we know.

To accept a myth as true is to believe that there is a correspondence between human meaning and a presumed universal order.
Myths fill the mysterious domain of the unknown and unknowable with more or less likely, but always intelligible, stories. In the
universe of myth nothing is meaningless: everything has its significant place. But since it is not possible to know whether there is, in
fact, such a correspondence, the claim to have discovered or related
it is itself a myth—that is, a tale that purports to convey knowledge of that which is not known. We conclude that the ultimate
meaning of myth is nothing less than the myth of meaning itself—
a myth both necessary and fundamental to human existence.

The world of myth is a world replete with meaning. The
mythical world-view knows nothing of those disjunctions between
meaning and existence, consciousness and reality, hope and expectation that the differentiating path of consciousness will reveal. Experience and reality are almost identical, for even that which goes
beyond experience—the realm opened to consciousness by the
quest for the origin of things—is filled with entities whose imag-

15. Mircea Eliade, "Methodological Remarks on the Study of Religious Symbolism," in Mircea Eliade and Joseph M. Kitagawa (eds.), *The History of Religions:
Essays in Method* (Chicago, 1959), 98.

ined characteristics are drawn from life. Life itself is the clue to the nature of the cosmos. Man sees everything as a living part—a partner—of a living whole. This conception of things is so remote from modern cosmology that we need to remind ourselves that there was a time before man discovered the existence of truly inanimate, "dead" matter. As Hans Jonas says, the concept of inorganic matter, so familiar to us,

> is anything but obvious. That the world is alive is really the most natural view, and largely supported by prima-facie evidence. On the terrestrial scene, in which experience is reared and contained, life abounds and occupies the whole foreground exposed to man's immediate view. The proportion of manifestly lifeless matter encountered in this primordial field is small, since most of what we now know to be inanimate is so intertwined with the dynamics of life that it seems to share its nature. Earth, wind and water—begetting, teeming, nurturing, destroying—are anything but models of "mere matter." Thus primitive panpsychism, in addition to answering powerful needs of the soul, was justified by rules of inference and verification within the available range of evidence, continually confirmed as it was by the actual preponderance of life in the horizon of its earthly home. Indeed not before the Copernican revolution widened this horizon into the vastness of cosmic space was the proportional place of life in the scheme of things sufficiently dwarfed so that it became possible to disregard it for most of what was henceforth to be the content of the term "nature." But to early man, standing on his earth arched by the dome of its sky, it could never occur that life might be a side issue in the universe and not its pervading rule. His panvitalism was a perspective truth which only a change of perspective could eventually displace. Unquestioned and convincing at the beginning stands the experience of the omnipresence of life."[16]

The force of this experience means that for countless centuries until the Renaissance, the predominant categories that men used to make sense of the universe were drawn from the living world. The development of philosophy and early science broke the compactness of this original world-view but did not radically call into question the central importance of life and purpose in the cosmos.

16. Hans Jonas, *The Phenomenon of Life: Toward a Philosophical Biology* (New York, 1966), 7–8.

The pre-Socratic philosophers distinguished between organic and inorganic nature but sought the source of both in a single vital principle that might be distinct from the universe or embedded within it. In the first case, a single ordering or creative god was postulated; in the second, a variety of pantheism or at least pan-psychism was implied. In their different ways, the Greek philosophers and the Hebrew prophets transformed the mythical world-view and emptied the world of the gods and spirits that had peopled it before, but neither seriously questioned that the origins of life and nonlife alike must lie in a living being. That is why the interpretation of the nature of things was governed above all by the category of purpose such as only a living being could process. The explanation of the world and of every being within it lay in the purpose for which it had been created or which it served in the economy of the whole.

Since the Renaissance our conception of nature has been utterly altered. Life is no longer a principle of explanation but something to be explained in terms of nonliving forms and forces. Chance and necessity, rooted alike in the mutually convertible properties of energy and matter, have displaced purpose. There are many varieties of this view, but they share the assurance that the emergent properties of life, consciousness, and spirit demand explanation in terms of less complex entities. Not everyone believes that everything is ultimately explicable in terms of the categories of physics. Biologists and sociobiologists, for instance, have a vested interest in defending the proposition that the systemic properties of organisms defy, for the present at least, any resolution into simpler units. But at every level of investigation the claim is made that the logic of explanation leads one way from lower to higher, simple to complex. Such claims are of course resisted. If biologists resist the encroachments of biochemists, sociologists no less resist those of sociobiologists. There are powerful arguments against reductionism, not least that the categories of the "lower" science—lower only in terms of the complexity of its object—give us less information than those devised by the "higher" in the course of investigation. But although these are effective arguments, they lack a justification in principle so long as they are not based in an ontology that recognizes the relative autonomy of the various strata of being and justifies this recognition by rational argument. We have to show that the prejudice in favor of simplicity, which is manifest in physical and biological reductionism no less than in the panvitalism of archaic ontology, is always misleading because the world itself is a complex of strata, each of which can only be understood in its own terms—terms that include an examination of its particular mode of dependence on the lower strata that support it. From such an ontology, promised but unachieved by Scheler and realized after his death by Nicolai Hartmann, we may hope to derive a realistic conception of the space of politics, the nature of political activity, and the limits of freedom.

To conclude this chapter I return to a direct examination of the relationship between nature and human nature. The experience of nature, whether articulated in myth or in modern evolutionary theory, is the experience of a process in which we have a more or less precarious place. But this process has a peculiar feature in that it is not intelligible in terms of pure or formless flux. Rather, it is one in which identifiable items emerge, beings that manifest substantially identical properties over time. If Darwinian teaching is accepted, then evolutionary change comes about as a result of chance mutation. This is not a continuous occurrence, and even if it were, the success of any mutant—its chance to win itself a place in the world—depends upon its environmental fitness. So long as the environment is not itself transformed, this means that there is great stability in the features of any given population. Thus nature, in the sense of essence—human nature, for example—is not banished from our vocabulary by the discovery that species are not created unchanging once and for all. Nature is a process in which "natures" emerge and crystallize until by chance or design they change or disappear. The time-scale of such transformations is, in general, so vast as to be practically irrelevant to the investigations of the human sciences, though not, as we shall see, to the requirements of a critically adequate ontology. It is not mere superstition that leads us to claim specific identity with our ancestors and descendants, nor obscurantism that requires us to investigate the characteristics of the finite nature of man.

Two

THE SPACE OF POLITICS

When man considers his nature and place in the cosmos he discovers that he is a free yet finite being. His freedom is real but limited. Human life is lived in tension between freedom and necessity, between what we may and what we must do and be. So we may conceive the world as a stage on which man is cast to play a particular, apparently important role in a drama of unknown length and significance. From the standpoint of the individual actor, the stage is set long before he makes his entrance in a scene already buzzing with life. He learns what his part is to be only from his fellow actors and from the opportunities for improvisation afforded him by their maneuvers and by the dimensions of the stage. If the ultimate significance of the drama escapes him, he is given, or at least believes himself to be given, certain uncertain clues. Rumors concerning such matters abound among the cast. The actor finds that he or some of his fellows seem to be able to control the direction in which the plot is leading. He knows with all the certainty of experience that the stage is not a uniform place. Sometimes it is more pleasant than others. At every time, some actors find more rewarding roles than the rest.

Theater itself is an excellent medium for the exploration of the metaphor of life as drama. In Tom Stoppard's *Rosencrantz and Guildenstern Are Dead,* Shakespeare's hapless courtiers are made the center of the audience's attention while remaining, as they were in *Hamlet,* far from the controlling springs of action that will seal their fate. The tragedy that is glimpsed occasionally when the

pair encounter and are commanded by the more potent characters
in Shakespeare's play provides the determining context for the public comedy and private tragedy of Rosencrantz and Guildenstern as
they try to puzzle out what is happening and how or if they may
take control of their destinies: "We have not been . . . picked out
. . . simply to be abandoned . . . set loose to find our own way. . . .
We are entitled to some direction . . . I would have thought."
"Wheels have been set in motion, and they have their own pace, to
which we are . . . condemned. Each move is dictated by the previous one—that is the meaning of order. If we start being arbitrary
it'll just be a shambles: at least let us hope so. Because if we happened, just happened to discover, or even suspect, that our sponta-
neity was part of their order, we'd know that we were lost."[1]
     The fate of Rosencrantz and Guildenstern is sealed, and the
audience knows it, because their world is the known drama of
Hamlet, whose outcome nothing can alter. The fate of the audience is, so far as its members can tell, relatively open and dependent upon decisions that have yet to be made as well as circumstances whose resolution cannot be foreseen. The human
perspective is not the eye of eternity, and even if, from that point,
everything *is* determined, then the logic of determination still remains itself unknown and unknowable. In order to be known sufficiently to negate the experience of freedom, to prove it a delusion,
the drama of existence would have to be known, if not from eternity, at least from its conclusion, and that precisely is what we do
not know. Freedom is unavoidable and irreducible. At the same
time, it is not unlimited. The investigations of philosophical anthropology confirm common experience in showing that a degree
of freedom is implicit in the relationship between nature and human nature. Man cannot but improvise essential elements of his
life through response to the circumstances in which he finds himself. What he produces must make sense to him, and so the stage
is filled with the works of consciousness—structures of meaning
and action that articulate man's response to the tension that holds
him and draws him to the ground on which he stands and to awareness of the ultimate ground of being that alone could explain his
situation.

---

1. Tom Stoppard, *Rosencrantz and Guildenstern Are Dead* (London, 1967).

But before we examine how the space of politics is filled we must examine how it is constituted. What is the structure of the reality that permits such a range of achievement to one of its constituent parts? To what is man responding when he constructs the political realm, as construct it he must? Philosophical anthropology cannot alone answer these questions. We must alter the focus of inquiry to fix not on the uniqueness of man but upon the general character of the real. Our concerns are properly ontological. In this chapter I shall, using the supple but systematic ontology developed by Nicolai Hartmann, try to make explicit the philosophical assumptions underlying our conception of politics as a realm of real but limited freedom. In an important sense Hartmann's is a limited ontology. He talks of it as a "new ontology," thereby opposing it to the old ontology that he, a neo-Kantian as much as a phenomenologist, regards as flawed by its implication with illegitimate—that is, critically untenable—metaphysical speculation on questions of ultimate origins and destiny that fall outside the range of possible knowledge. Thus this study of the general character of the real—being as being—is from the beginning a creature of man's effort to answer the question of his and the world's origin and destiny. The roots of metaphysics are sunk in the same soil as those of myth, and—man's concerns and capacities being what they are—the temptation to confuse mere plausibility with truth is always present. Hartmann follows Kant in rejecting the philosophical legitimacy of all such speculations. What they reveal cannot be more than a range of plausible possibilities between which critically justified choice is impossible. We must, he insists, respect the *aporias*—the impassable perplexities bounding the field of human knowledge but not imagination.

But the field of what, since St. Thomas Aquinas, has been called "metaphysics" is divisible. The Jesuit thinker Francisco Suárez distinguished general metaphysics from what he called "special metaphysics." The former is the study of all *possible* being; the latter, of *actual* being. It is the second that constitutes the legitimate field of ontology in Hartmann's sense. Ontology is empirically based in our experience of the world as the necessary, intentional object of knowledge. Its topic is the structure of real—that is, temporally and, with important exceptions, spatially existent—and ideal—that is, intelligible—being, and its mode of investigation is a study

of the categories which, at different levels of being, govern the behavior of items encountered in experience. Its purpose is the prepa-
ration of an admittedly provisional but well-corroborated account
of the stage on which our lives are set.

Concern with ontology is bound to have important consequences
for our conception of the human sciences. It has been rightly
stressed by many authors that the human world is constituted by
actions that are meaningful to those who carry them out. To understand society, we must grasp the meaning that the social actors
attach to their actions. Using the insights of Alfred Schutz, Paul
Ricoeur, and others, I have argued elsewhere that such understanding is necessarily indirect and mediated by interpretation of the
symbols through which meaning is expressed.[2] Human studies are
therefore necessarily hermeneutic disciplines whose appropriate
form of inquiry owes more to the logic of textual interpretation
than to the commonly accepted models of natural science. But her-
meneutics—the interpretation of meaning—has its own horizon,
as Hartmann implies when he writes: "the activity of man, spiritual life and historical actuality, can by no means be adequately
grasped by an understanding of meaning. With this concept we are
still in the air, with no firm ground under our feet. We shall have
to return to comprehension based upon knowledge of laws. For the
firm ground on which spirit rests is not itself spirit, nor even anything of its kind, but just what is opposite and foreign to it, the
wide realm of nature, in the first place organic nature, but indirectly also inorganic nature."[3]

Inorganic nature, organic nature, consciousness, and spirit form,
according to Hartmann, the four strata of real being. Consciousness
and spirit—which Hartmann identifies with the man-made but
supraindividual reality of culture—depend upon the lower strata
and are, in their turn, the bearers of ideal beings such as numbers
and values. The latter exist only in the media of consciousness or
spirit but are in themselves autonomous in essence. Dependency
does not imply determination. Organic life depends upon material
relations between inorganic atoms, as psychic and spiritual life de-

2. David J. Levy, *Realism: An Essay in Interpretation and Social Reality* (Manchester, 1981).
3. Nicolai Hartmann, *New Ways of Ontology*, trans. Reinhard C. Kuhn (Chicago,
1952), 34.

pends upon the organism, but "such a dependency in no way excludes autonomy. . . . It must only be granted that the *conditio sine qua non* of the higher forms of being is always provided by the lower forms and, in the last analysis, by the entire series of lower forms."[4] The phrase *conditio sine qua non* draws our attention to the fact that in talking of the ontology of human existence we are speaking of the conditions that are necessary but not sufficient for the emergence of the achieved forms of cultural life and political order. The order delineated by ontology is the precondition of history and politics, and forms, at every time, the frontier beyond which activity cannot pass. But this determines only the limits of action, never the content of positive achievement.

Emergence is a vague term, and frustration at our inability to pin down its exact meaning in the process of the world and the formation of types within it combines with intellectual prejudice in favor of simplicity to recommend a determinist conception of dependence for which we have in experience very little evidence. Physical or biological determinism explains, in fact, hardly anything of the known variety of human achievement and nothing of the nature of psychic and cultural experience. If determinism appeals to the mind, it is because it seems more coherent than other views and not because it corresponds to anything in mental life. Moreover, since we can hardly doubt that inorganic and organic nature provide the foundation and cosmic context for all such experience, and since our understanding of these strata is commonly couched in terms of necessary causal laws relating initial conditions to determined consequences, it seems an act of intellectual, even moral, weakness and sentimentality to cut the chain of causality just at the point where it threatens to throttle our prized sense of autonomy. One of the virtues of Hartmann's conception of the world as a unity of heterogeneous strata, each governed by its own categorical systems that cannot without close examination be transferred to other strata, is that it allows us to reconcile the apparently conflicting experiences of causal dependence and autonomy without any sacrifice of intellectual rigor.

There are three major problem areas in this ontology. First, it

4. *Ibid.*, 36.

must develop a nondeterminist conception of ontological dependence between strata. Second, it must delineate the categories that
are specific to particular strata as well as those that connect them.
And third, it must, in consequence of the findings of the first two,
show how the various strata are related not only in the broad world
picture but within the higher beings that emerge within it. It is
characteristic of the four ontologically distinguishable strata that

> they not only do not coincide with the levels of actual structures
> (inanimate object, organism, man, and so on) but rather cut across
> them. They are not only strata of the real world as a totality but also
> strata of the actual structures themselves. Man, for example, is not
> only a spirit; he has a spiritless, psychic life too. He is also an organ-
> ism and is even a material structure of the same nature as other in-
> animate things. He reacts to certain stimuli instinctively like an ani-
> mal, and, like an animal, too, he propagates his species, just as he
> experiences thrust and counter-thrust like a material object. The or-
> ganism, for its part, possesses, beside the quality of being animate,
> also the general character of physical materiality. Indeed, only thus
> is it possible that the organism's life process should consist essen-
> tially in a change of materials. Nonetheless, looked at ontologically,
> the organism consists of only two strata, while man embraces all
> four strata. In the higher reaches of the animal kingdom the three-
> fold division already begins to manifest itself inasmuch as the emer-
> gence of consciousness adds another level to organic life. . . . The
> tiers of reality form a stratified order not only within the unity of
> the world but also in the actual structures of the higher layers, in
> such a fashion that the lower strata are always included in the higher
> ones. And this relation obviously cannot be reversed. The organism
> cannot exist without atoms and molecules, but these can exist with-
> out the organism.[5]

The identification of the categories characteristic of each layer is
an empirical task based in acquaintance with real structures.
Thus, for example, we find that the categories of animate nature—
organic structure, adaptation and purposiveness, metabolism, self-
regulation, self-restoration, the life of the species, the constancy of

5. *Ibid.*, 48.

the species, and variation—are not to be found in the inorganic
layer whose existence that of the organism presupposes. They do,
on the other hand, recur in modified form in higher beings possessed of psychic or spiritual life. Generally, then, the pattern governing the occurrence of ontologically specific categories is that,
while the categories of the lower stratum play their part in the constitution of the higher, the reverse does not happen. The abiding
fault of every metaphysical theory that purports to interpret all
reality in terms of psychic categories like intention and purpose
lies, according to Hartmann, in its failure to recognize this pattern.
   Time, process, and causality—the most universal of categories
found initially at the level of the inorganic—penetrate all the
higher strata. Space, which we commonly regard alongside time as
an equivalent coordinate of reality, is not, in contrast, a feature of
consciousness or of spirit.

   The difference in the behavior of the various categories prevents recurrence from becoming a universal law. It is confined to a limited
   number of categories. Yet there is no complete lack of rules. On the
   basis of the sequence of strata it can be shown that the breaking off
   of certain groups of pervasive categories takes place only at certain
   levels. Such a level is the borderline between the organic and the
   psychic. Here the situation is different from the one prevailing at the
   frontiers between inanimate nature and the organism. The categories of the inorganic all penetrate into the realm of the organic, although some of them play only a very insignificant role there. The
   reason for this is that the organism includes as integral parts the
   dynamic structures of masses ordered to one another, superinform-
   ing these structures by virtue of its own more elevated structure.
   Along with these inferior structures it also appropriates their categories. . . . This relation of "superinformation" is, however, not typical of the "distance" between strata. The psychic life is not superinformation of corporeal life. It does not integrate the organic
   processes and does not use them as integral parts. It is supported by
   these organic processes and influenced by them. But they continue
   below it. There may be a consciousness of metabolism or growth,
   but only in the sense in which there is a consciousness of external
   objects and processes. These, as objects of the consciousness, are lo-

cated outside the consciousness. Neither as acts nor as content do they become part of its existence. . . . Act and content are of categorically different kind. They possess neither spatiality, nor even substantiality. The "inner world" which is built out of them—the world of experience, feeling, perception, thinking—is an ontological region "above" organic structure, but it only rests "upon" it as on its ontological basis. It does not consist "of it" as of its material. In contradistinction to superinformation, this relation of one stratum put on top of another may be styled "superimposition."[6]

The borderline between psychic and spiritual life, between personal consciousness and objective spirit, is also only definable in these terms:

> . . . the historical life of the objective spirit does not consist of psychic acts but only "rests" on them. . . . Speech, legal order, custom, morality and science are more than parts of a consciousness. The individual receives them from the common spiritual sphere of which he becomes a participant, and then hands them on. He contributes his share to their total historical process, but he does not create for himself his own speech, morality or science. Correspondingly, the spiritual world does not form the content of a superpersonal consciousness as is believed by some metaphysical theories. Consciousness exists only as the consciousness of the individual, but this is no adequate consciousness of the objective spirit. Besides their common racial origin, the individuals are tied together only by their common spiritual world. Every human being has his psychic life incontestably for himself. Nobody else can act or suffer for him. Consciousness divides; the spirit unites.[7]

Even lengthy quotation can do only scant justice to the subtlety of Hartmann's analysis, which depends so much upon the sustained arguments and the anticipation of objections that his book contains. It seems to me that the ontology that he proposes allows us to resolve many of the problems posed by simultaneous awareness of our freedom from and dependence upon the world. It gives precise intellectual content to the notion of relative autonomy

6. *Ibid.*, 78–79.
7. *Ibid.*, 80.

or finite freedom—a notion necessary to the accurate registration
of our experience as human beings but which, without ontological
clarification, seems intellectually evasive and even unintelligible.
More than this, it offers us a convincing account of the synthetic
nature of man as a unity of heterogeneous strata, and of the relationships of the world of culture to the acts and conditions that
support and sustain it. It offers guidance as to how we should conceive the freedom of the finite, contingent being that is man—a
being who not only constructs the polity in the context of a pre-
existing cosmos but does so with mental and material resources
that are, as much as the context, a part of his inheritance. Finally,
it provides us with a defensible way of viewing the relationship
between what we can call the subjective and objective dimensions
of political order—the meaning and function of institutions that
can only function in the human world because they mean something to those who act in and through them. The relative autonomy of the life of the psyche and spirit is the very lifeblood
of an order that is at best dimly suggested by the biological inheritance we share as members of the human race. If the possibility of
political order is a function of our specific biological identity, its
actualization is a matter of spiritual, cultural coherence—a bringing together of individual psyches in the shared traditions of a historically formed culture.

Theoretical inquiry, exemplified here by Hartmann's ontology,
is not empirical investigation, nor is it empty fictive speculation
multiplying imagined entities to explain otherwise puzzling experiences. It starts in mundane experience and cannot directly expand man's experiential range. It offers no alternative to the discoveries of natural science. Nonetheless, it is an invaluable—perhaps
the most precious—part of human knowledge. For theoretical inquiry alone allows us to discover the significance of what empirical
investigation reveals. It does this through the critical development
of distinctions necessary to an adequate understanding of the real.
Theoretical sophistication is not a gift of nature. The most brilliant
scientist may hold a view of the world which, while more coherent
and better corroborated than that of the untutored layman, is no
less compact and inadequate to the understanding of the complexity of the real. Typically, the specialist "expert" who aspires to

dispense universal wisdom in print or on the screen seeks to explain everything in terms of the province of the real with which he
is most familiar, or at the least with categories and forms of explanation derived from that field. The result is a reductionist conception of the nature of things which, because it has the prestige
of "hard science" and offers a single key to unlock the enigmas of
the world, may achieve widespread popularity. The popularization
of ethology in the brilliantly written books of Robert Ardrey in the
1960s and the more recent vogue of primers of sociobiology show
us the consequences.

    Neither the data concerning human origins, which provided the
starting point for Ardrey, nor the investigations of contemporary
genetics, which fuel sociobiology, warrant the reductionist conclusions that are commonly drawn from them. On the other hand,
these authors' overestimation of the consequences of these discoveries—the claim that they alone explain human nature and society—provokes a predictable ideological reaction from those committed to the view that our biological inheritance is irrelevant to
our political needs and aspirations. Even a writer like Edward O.
Wilson, who repeatedly emphasizes that sociobiology is not determinist in its implications, cannot avoid identifying theoretical
clarification with the logic of reduction, as when he seeks to explain religious practices in terms of biological advantage.[8] Konrad
Lorenz, in contrast, presents a more adequate, because more philosophically informed, reading of the relationship between the bio-
logical/natural and the cultural/spiritual factors in human existence. Wilson enters the field of philosophical anthropology as a
geneticist properly scandalized by the ignorance and suspicion of
his important subject displayed by those who describe themselves
as social scientists. But such a background does not by itself make
a man a proper judge of the real significance of the enlightenment
that his expertise can bring in matters otherwise obscure. The significance of ontological distinctions is not obvious to those unfamiliar with writers specifically concerned with distinctively philosophical—that is, theoretical rather than empirical—issues in
the study of man's place in the cosmos. Here, I think, Lorenz, the

----

8. Edward O. Wilson, *On Human Nature* (New York, 1979).

reader and critic of Plessner, Gehlen, and Hartmann, has the advantage over one who, like Wilson, comes from a tradition in which philosophers have, until recently and with noted exceptions like Whitehead, been content merely to launder the concepts that form the working habit of the natural-scientific professions.

Thus in his book *Behind the Mirror,* subtitled *A Search for a Natural History of Human Knowledge,* Lorenz prefaces his investigation of the emergence of the unique yet scientifically intelligible human mind with the following passage from Hartmann:

> Organic nature rises above inorganic nature—not freely and independently, however, but on the basis of the laws and circumstances of the world of matter, even though these laws and circumstances are far from sufficient in themselves to constitute life. Likewise spiritual life and consciousness have as their prerequisite an organism in which and with which they come into the world. In like manner the great historical moments in cultural, spiritual life are carried by the conscious life of the individuals involved. From stratum to stratum, passing across the successive divisions, we find everywhere the principle of dependence upon the stratum with its own structures and laws. This relationship constitutes the real unity of the actual world. For all its variety and heterogeneity, the world is still an entity. It has the unity of a system—a system of different strata. The vital point is not that the differences between these levels are unbridgeable—indeed, it· may only be to us that they appear unbridgeable—but that new laws and categories are established which, though dependent on those of the strata below, have their own character and assert their own autonomy.

On which Lorenz comments: "For me the most convincing proof of the correctness of Hartmann's views is that, although they take not the slightest account of the facts of evolution, they tally absolutely with these facts, just as any sound system of comparative anatomy does, even if it belongs to pre-Darwinian days. Hartmann's sequence of strata corresponds directly to the pattern of evolution: there was inorganic matter on earth long before organic life; much later central nervous systems with a capacity for subjective experience, a 'soul,' evolved; finally, only in the most recent phase of creation did the spiritual life of human culture make its appearance."[9]

There is more to the Lorenz/Hartmann relationship than the pat on the back offered by the scientist to the philosopher. Lorenz recognizes that the structural analysis of ontology delineates the outline of the real world whose history evolution purports to explain. Ontology portrays the anatomy of actuality—the structure of the world's body—as natural science alone cannot do. Reference to Hartmann's work testifies to Lorenz's awareness that, while evolutionary theory hypothetically explains the development of species and their defining features, the laws governing phylogenetic developments do not tell us what is the place of each being in the whole or the balance of factors within each. Lorenz's views on human society have provoked considerable controversy because of his emphasis on the importance of aggression in human life, a feature he traces to our ancestry. But a much more significant feature of his thought seems to me to be the way he treats the cultural world, including the sphere of politics, as a relatively autonomous, humanly created, spiritually formed realm constructed in the space allowed it by the operation of the lower strata.

This is of particular importance for our understanding of the significance of continuity and tradition in human life. The liberty allowed us by our nature and place in the universe does not mean that our species does not, like every other, require constancy in its environment. What it does mean is that constancy must be created and incessantly re-created through the formation and maintenance of institutions that effectively limit the range of conceivable options for the individual. Following Arnold Gehlen, himself influenced by Scheler and Hartmann, I argue, first, that institutional stability is of prime importance for a species whose biological inheritance is sufficient to give it material and spiritual needs but insufficient to provide for them, and, second, that social existence is only possible so long as everything is not called into question every day. There is a dialectic of freedom and order in human affairs. Freely we must create and sustain the order that limits freedom: only in such an order can freedom be anything more than an

9. Konrad Lorenz, *Behind the Mirror: A Search for a Natural History of Human Knowledge*, trans. Ronald Taylor (London, 1976), 38.

abstraction. In the words of Edmund Burke: "Society cannot exist unless a controlling power upon will and appetite be placed somewhere, and the less of it there is within, the more there must be without. It is ordained in the eternal constitution of things, that men of intemperate minds cannot be free. Their passions forge their fetters."[10]

This position is not the consequence but the precondition of history. Human existence is historical existence only because of the dimension of freedom and spirit that is allowed it in the space of politics. Because we construct the order that nature compels us to inhabit—construct it formally as well as materially—political order has a history in a way that the order of the anthill has not. There is a prehistory to every insect society, which is the story of the origins of the species whose existence is crystallized in the structurally static dynamism of the hill or hive, but there is no history. The chronicles of the anthill would tell of battles lost and won and of natural obstacles encountered and overcome. They would have nothing of the substance of human history, which is found in man's effort to comprehend his nature and situation, to attune himself to it in a fashion that maximizes the potential that, for the time being, he believes himself to have. History is the proving ground of all such beliefs. Because it is an open-ended process—a mystery in process of unfolding—knowledge of the being whose nature is articulated through it is neither complete nor secure. It is incomplete because knowledge of the process is incomplete. It is insecure because it is easier to forget than to recover the insights that are from time to time painfully achieved. This, I shall argue, is the root of the problem of ideology. What distinguishes political philosophy from ideology is the comprehensiveness of its grounding in critical clarification of the necessary conditions of human existence. It is desirable but not always essential to make our understanding of the structure of this ground explicit. However, it becomes essential to do so when the nature of the grounding and the ground come to be radically misconceived. An explicit philosophical anthropology and ontology are today the necessary prologue to political, theoretical inquiry.

10. Louis I. Bredvold and Ralph G. Ross (eds.), *The Philosophy of Edmund Burke: A Selection from His Speeches and Writings* (Ann Arbor, Mich., 1961).

It was not always so. So long as man lived in immediate dependence upon nature, there was a native realism in the common sense
that his environment imposed upon him. His myths might be fantastic, but they could not be absolutely misleading, for they were,
broadly speaking, tied to his efforts to account for the position of
finitude in which he found himself. If they went beyond this, man
paid an immediate price for forgetting his place. Today this condition no longer holds. It is not that man's nature or ontological condition has been transformed, but that his use of the power that he
possesses to alter and improve his way of life has placed him in
a state where the truth of his finitude, let alone its extent, is no
longer obvious. He fantasizes that he has no nature, that his is a
form of being so open that anything is possible to it, that political
order may itself be transcended in a future without institutional
support or constraint. Ideology in its strong sense involves the
belief that political means may be used to deliver us from the demands of politics. This belief is so important a component in the
contemporary crisis of political order that it will be examined in
a separate chapter. However, no discussion of the space of politics
would be complete without an examination of the state of affairs
that gives this mistaken view its apparent plausibility. The defor-
mation and ultimate denial of ontological truth by ideology can be
left for later discussion. The existential state that makes it socially
effective must be examined here, for it is a constitutive feature of
the human stage today.

What I have in mind is the massive shift in the material make-
up of the environment that has happened in industrially advanced
societies over the last couple of centuries. The space of politics, I
suggested, is the realm opened up to man by the incompleteness of
his instinctual equipment, his capacity for reflective and projective
thought, and the opportunities afforded him by the inherent possibilities of inorganic and organic nature. The relationship of such
a being to the world is more practical than theoretical. Practical
intelligence, applied to the satisfaction of a felt need, is shared
by man with the higher animals. It precedes critical reflection. We
should not imagine that practical intelligence in man consists only
of a capacity for developing techniques for the control of the material world. It is also the driving force in the construction of the

inclusive-meaning patterns that are represented by myth. Myths make the world a home for man as surely as the techniques with which he builds his material shelters. The need for meaning is as basic as the need for sustenance or sexual satisfaction in a being like man, who cannot act effectively without self-consciously considering the positions in which he finds himself.

It is, however, the more narrowly practical consequences of the work of practical reason that I want to consider here, for these result in the steady build-up of an environmental layer produced by the application of an ever more sophisticated technology which, as it were, interposes a cushion of man-made objects between ourselves and the cosmos that supports us. Arnold Gehlen has analyzed this process with considerable subtlety:

Ultimately, all attainments of the human mind remain enigmatic; but the enigma would be all the more impenetrable if not seen in connection with man's organic and instinctual deficiencies; for his intellect relieves him from the necessity to undergo organic adaptations to which animals are subject, and conversely allows him to alter his original circumstances to suit himself. If by technique we understand the capacities and means whereby man puts nature to his own service, by identifying nature's properties and laws in order to exploit them and to control their interaction, clearly technique, in this highly general sense, is part and parcel of man's very essence. . . . Over the ages, the tendency to replace missing organs has reached beyond the sphere of the body, and penetrated into deeper and deeper organic strata. The replacement of the organic by the inorganic constitutes one of the most significant outcomes of the development of culture. There are two aspects to this tendency: artificial materials replacing those organically produced; and non-organic energy replacing organic energy. As to the former, the development of metallurgy constitutes a cultural threshold of the first magnitude; we speak of the Bronze Age, Iron Age, etc. Metals replace and outperform materials immediately available in the environment, particularly stone and wood. As late as the Middle Ages ships, bridges, vehicles, and tools were largely made of woods, and no other fuel was known. Today, concrete, metals, coke, coal, and numerous synthetic materials have largely supplanted wood, and car bodies made of plastic may soon replace those made of steel. Leather and hemp have been replaced by steel cables, wax candles by gas or electricity, indigo and purple by aniline dyes, nearly all natural drugs and medicinal herbs by synthetic products.[11]

Man's state of dependence on what is not himself is disguised but not negated by his creation of an "artificial nature" constructed in the image of his subjective requirements. The second aspect of this tendency—the supplanting of organic by inorganic energy sources with the development of the steam engine and the internal combustion engine—further loosens, but again does not negate, our dependence upon that which is not ourselves. Coal and oil are, of course, legacies of past organic life,

> yet they entail a key transformation: as far as energy sources are concerned, mankind has made itself independent of those that are renewed from year to year. As long as wood remained the most significant fuel material, and the work of domestic animals the most important source of energy, the advance of material culture, and thus ultimately population growth, met a limit of a non-technical kind that rested upon the slow tempo of organic growth and reproduction. By building hydroelectric power stations and by gaining control over nuclear energy, man has freed his energy supplies from the limitations of the renewal of organic substances.[12]

A further crucial aspect of this tendency of man to displace himself from nature is the spread of a worldwide communications and information network. The range of information provided and the impossibility of our checking it against personal experience means that, once again, a man-made layer is interposed between us and the facts of life. Whatever the intent behind it, the technology of communication means that reality is processed for our consumption in analogous fashion to the processing of food and fibers. Like the latter, the resulting "news" may be more or less wholesome, depending upon how the processors conceive their responsibilities and what they take to be the needs of consumers. It is obvious that

11. Arnold Gehlen, *Man in the Age of Technology*, trans. Patricia Lipscomb (New York, 1980), 4–5.
12. *Ibid.*, 6.

this situation is full of opportunities for ideological distortion, and that the general distancing of man from a level of experience whose truth is beyond effective manipulation makes it difficult for him to discover when this is happening. Some conclude that, distortion being inevitable, all that can be done is to "slant" the news the "right" way. This is the characteristic position of social-revolutionary groups, and when put into practice its effect is to convert an ever-present risk into a hideous certainty.

The apparent solidity of man's artful environment, which also includes the network of established social institutions, makes it easy to forget that it is not the ultimate ground of existence. The existential state of technologically advanced modernity is itself no more than the embodiment of a certain cluster of possibilities of nature and human nature. The manipulation of nature is absolutely dependent upon our obedience to its causal structure. Thus the analysis of social structure and technological achievement is not the ultimate framework within which our picture of the social world of meaning is set. The ontology of human existence is not merely, or even most basically, an ontology of social being, taken to mean the limiting frame of political and economic institutions, for these too are generated in response to the demands of levels of reality that precede consciousness. We cannot even say—as structuralists are inclined to do—that the analysis of social structure represents a deeper level of understanding than the interpretation of meaning, for the level of structure bears everywhere the imprint of conscious purpose, although this is not always enough to define its function. Rather, we should say that the political order is an irreducible complex of meaningful action and cultural achievement. The latter, ontologically higher than consciousness and therefore dependent upon it, precedes every individual action. It belongs to the stratum of objective spirit beyond the immediate control of consciousness but resting upon it. Inconceivable and nonexistent without consciousness, the spiritual sphere of culture forms the historical stream in which alone human consciousness survives. The whole complex rests in its turn upon levels of being indifferent to, although not unaffected by, the artful creature who develops upon them.

Once more we turn to Hartmann for a clear statement of the

anthropological consequences of this ontological condition. The
recognition that reality is a unity of heterogeneous strata, in which
the nexus of causal determination operates variously depending
upon the level concerned, gives us a conception of human freedom
that delimits the space of politics.

> At every stage of the causal series there is a multiplicity of determin-
> ing factors which together constitute the components of a general
> resultant. None of them can be omitted, for each one depends on a
> whole chain of causes. But new components can be added. The group
> of components is no closed system. Rather it is receptive to every
> insertion by which a co-determining element is added to the deter-
> minative whole. This is clearly reflected in the indifference of the
> causal nexus toward the result. For every new component must, of
> course, deflect the general direction. . . . Were the world ordered
> teleologically from below upwards, man would be unable to develop
> any kind of activity. His purposes would be in no position to insert
> themselves into the course of events. But if the world is determined
> causally only, and if teleological determination is the prerogative of
> man, he is free to deflect processes within the limits of his under-
> standing of causality. For the causal chains admit as new compo-
> nents the purposes set by him, and they are given a sequence of causal
> effects in the same way as the indigenous components.[13]

Far from precluding human freedom, causality permits it. More
than this, it is its necessary condition, for only a world of regular
causality could be understood and provide an estimable context for
subjective choice and purpose: "Causal processes can be directed,
because they are not committed to final purposes but proceed in-
differently. It is true they are dirigible only if man recognizes their
laws and adapts himself to them. Once this condition is fulfilled
they offer no active resistance to his guidance. On the other hand,
if the world of things were not causally determined, man could
neither direct events nor realize goals. He would be unable to select
means towards his ends. For the selection is made with a view to
the causal effects of the means."[14]

This is the ontological basis on which free will depends and with

13. Hartmann, *New Ways of Ontology*, 131.
14. *Ibid.*, 132.

it the domain of political life and history. Beyond the structure of actuality that Hartmann analyzes so acutely remain the mysteries of ultimate origin and destiny. But just as our conception of human reality cannot be limited to what men control or produce, so we must not go to the other extreme and ignore the necessities of actual being in the light of what we may, on extrascientific grounds however valid, believe concerning what is beyond the bounds of knowledge. Thomist metaphysics, as so eloquently restated in the work of Jacques Maritain, teaches, in explicit contrast to the ontology of Hartmann, that knowledge of creation leads necessarily to awareness of a divine creator. But even in this perspective such awareness cannot be allowed to falsify what we otherwise know to be true. The arguments of Thomist natural theology—as opposed to the theological articulation of specifically mystical experience—proceed from the experience of creation to awareness of the intelligible necessity of there being a transcendent creator. Natural theology is knowledge of divinity mediated by experience of the intelligible actuality of the cosmos. The world is what it is, even if we are led to the discovery of the one world-transcendent God as its source and ground. Consequently, the space of politics has a shape and inherent necessities of its own. It cannot be remade in the image of an absolute—even though that absolute be its ultimate divine creator—without denying the facts of creation itself.[15]

15. Jacques Maritain, *The Degrees of Knowledge*, trans. Bernard Wall and Margot R. Adamson (New York, 1959); David J. Levy, "Jacques Maritain, Thomism and Politics," *Occasional Review*, IV (1976), 35–65.

THREE

THE POLITICAL CONDITION

Within the perspective of philosophical anthropology, "political order" can be conceived in both a broad and a narrow sense. In the broad sense, it means the form of social existence characteristic of and necessary to a being whose genetically transmitted inheritance of instincts and behavioral patterns is insufficiently compelling or complete to determine the specific forms of its communal life. In the narrow sense, political order refers to the network of institutions that such a being must construct in order to regulate the relationships of power and subordination arising between the members of his species. In its broad sense, political order is descriptive of human society as such; while more narrowly it points to the naturally required but culturally constituted core of institutions that embody legitimate authority among men. The purpose of this chapter is to sketch the way in which political order, in its narrow as well as its broad sense, is a necessary requirement of human life, entailed in certain fundamental conditions of man's existence in the world. There is more to human life than politics, but, in a sense that I shall elucidate later, the human condition is essentially and ineradicably a political condition. This is the specific difference setting the social life of man apart from that of every other animal.

In arguing this point, I shall draw on the philosophical anthropological studies of Helmuth Plessner and Arnold Gehlen and on the work of Hans Jonas, whose project of a philosophical biology provides invaluable clues to the understanding of the phenomenon of finite freedom, the highest expression of which we find in the human world. Man's freedom, as Nicolai Hartmann reminds us, is "tied everywhere to conditions of realization which he did not create but which leave him an opening for his own initiative. . . . The real task of philosophy concerning the problem of freedom consists fundamentally in properly defining the limits of freedom. It must be understood as a freedom conditioned by manifold dependencies and maintaining itself against them. Otherwise philosophy would be dealing with the mere dream of freedom, not with its reality."[1] The fact that there have been those, from Rousseau in the eighteenth century to Sartre in the twentieth, who have considered only the dream of absolute autonomy to be worthy of the name of freedom makes it all the more important that we understand the real state of affairs.

Concern with ontology and the various biological and cultural constants identified by the philosophical anthropologists reflects a desire not to deny human freedom but to understand it for what it truly is. To understand anything pertaining to the real world involves understanding its place in the whole. Indeed, to say that something has such a place is another way of saying that it is real. It is also to say that it is finite, for every element in a situation must in some sense be conditioned by what surrounds it. Human freedom is no exception. Its reality is not assured by any futile attempt to break the chains that bind the nature of order to the order of nature, but by the legitimate argument that dependencies, however manifold, do not necessarily amount to thoroughgoing determination. There is nothing determined about political order except its necessity to man as a free, world-open being. If it has certain necessary structures, then even these must be understood as creative human accomplishments in the face of potential chaos.

Here we must distinguish between two senses in which men can be said to be free—the political and the ontological. Political freedom is an achievement of human history. It results whenever men are successful in constructing an institutional order suitable to their needs and able to defend itself from its potential enemies. Ontological freedom, in contrast, is no human achievement but a

1. Nicolai Hartmann, *New Ways of Ontology*, trans. Reinhard C. Kuhn (Chicago, 1952), 31.

condition of man beset by risks. As Plessner says, "Achieving life,
man himself as a living being first of all has to create the conditions
for life. Artifacts from the past are witness to the protective coating
with which man has surrounded himself and which is again and
again exposed to the threat of destruction." To speak of the human
condition as inherently political is to say that man must build consciously what is given complete to his fellow creatures: the world
he requires for his survival and fulfillment. He does this by constructing cultural patterns, institutions, and belief systems that
answer the need. "But what," Plessner asks, "are these comforting
patterns of our existence without the dimension of strangeness
against which they protect us, without a world which is somehow beyond our reach and perhaps ultimately unfathomable? Only
against the background of an open world transcending biological
constraints—a world which, prone to unexpected turns, urges him
into ever new and fragile compromises—is man able to maintain
the precarious and vulnerable balance of cultural life."[2]
    The simultaneous vulnerability and necessity of the cultural
realm goes far toward explaining the typically ambiguous way in
which man experiences and symbolizes the phenomenon of political order. On the one hand, he regards it as something willed by
the gods or continuous and compatible with the forces governing
the universe. On the other, he sees it as something fragile and foreign to the nature of things—a human enclosure erected in the face
of a chaos that would otherwise overwhelm him. Only careful examination of the nature and scope of man's finite freedom will
reveal the full significance of this ambiguity by describing the interplay of freedom and necessity in the political condition. The
ambiguity of experience and symbol will then be seen to correspond to the irreducible mystery that man presents to himself, for
it is the fate of a world-open being that, never being able to experience his full possibilities, he must construct an image of himself
that hides its fallibility in the common certainties of social con-
vention. Quoting Plessner once more:

2. Helmuth Plessner, "De Homine Abscondito," *Social Research*, XXXVI
(1969), 501; Helmuth Plessner, *Conditio Humana* (Pfullingen, 1964), quoted by
Fred R. Dallmayr in "Plessner's Philosophical Anthropology: Implications for Role
Theory and Politics," *Inquiry*, XVII (1974), 55.

The concealment of man from himself as well as from his fellow men—*homo absconditus*—is the somber side of his openness to the world. He can never discover himself completely in his actions—only his shadow which precedes him and remains behind him, an imprint, a clue to himself. Therefore man has history. He makes it and it makes him. His activities, forced on him because they make possible his mode of life, at the same time disclose to him and conceal from him the interpretation of events, which not only depend on some initial constellation of circumstances, but also on their effects which are open to an incalculable future.[3]

The full ambiguity and pathos of finite freedom are revealed only in the human sphere, but, though unique in its extent and in the way it is exercised, man's freedom is prefigured in the mode of existence of any organism, however primitive. Hans Jonas argues that a certain freedom is intrinsic to the phenomenon of life itself, and this argument is significant for our inquiry. If political order is the constitutive form of human freedom—the necessary framework for the life of such a being as man—it is important to understand what finite freedom involves. To follow the spoor of freedom upward through the levels of organic life to man will serve to remind us that the reality of freedom has little in common with the dream of absolute autonomy, which finds expression in the belief that man could one day live a truly "free" life beyond the disputes and constraints of political order.

In the light of technological developments in communications and genetic engineering, it would be foolish to deny that some parody of this fantasy of postpolitical existence is historically possible. The point is that it could not represent an advance beyond political order to a higher, freer level of being but would have to take the form of an induced reversion to the prereflective totalitarianism of organically transmitted instinct. The means by which the imperative of conformity would be communicated might be new, but the result would be, sociologically speaking, as old as the anthill. We can retreat behind freedom but we cannot advance beyond it; and the freedom that is man's has institutional order as its essential correlate. This is the particular human case of the general

3. Plessner, "De Homine Abscondito," 503.

law that governs living things, that the activity of every living being must directly or indirectly maintain the balance between itself
and the sort of world that makes its continued existence possible.
The political condition is one in which this balance, no longer assured by the limiting framework of organic metabolism and animal
instinct, becomes the responsibility of the conscious action of
men. This is the insight that underlies Gehlen's theory of institutions, according to which social institutions, at once enabling and
limiting human function, fulfill for man the role taken by biological structures in the life of other species.[4]

In what, though, does the primordial freedom of the organism
consist? To answer this, we must first ask what gives anything its
identity over time. In the case of the inorganic, there is no problem:
its identity consists in the sameness of the parts composing it. It
is, in Jonas' words, "the collection of the identities of all its simultaneous member units while they travel together through space-
time. Wishing to ascertain . . . whether a body has stayed 'the same'
between two observations the physicist would ideally have to put
identifying marks on all of its atoms and check on the later occasion whether it still consists of all the marked ones and of no
others. Barring evidence to the contrary, this is taken for granted,
and weighing the mass is deemed a significant control."[5]

The case of the organism, which survives by metabolizing elements of its environment, is different. Metabolism—the process by
which nutritive material is built up into living matter or by which
protoplasm is broken down into simpler substances to perform special functions—changes the matter of which the parts of the organism are composed. Indeed, the organism only remains the same—a
living rather than a dead being—so long as this transformation of
elements continues. "We are faced," says Jonas,

> with the ontological (not only epistemological) fact of an identity
> totally different from physical identity. . . . On the one hand the liv-
> ing being is a composite matter, and at any time its reality totally
> coincides with its contemporary stuff—that is with one definite

4. Peter Berger and Hansfried Kellner, "Arnold Gehlen and the Theory of Institutions," *Social Research*, XXXII (1965), 110–15.
5. Hans Jonas, "Biological Foundations of Individuality," in Hans Jonas, *Philosophical Essays: From Ancient Creed to Technological Man* (Englewood Cliffs, N.J.,
1974), 189–90.

manifold of individual components. On the other hand, it is not identical with this or any such simultaneous total, and its reality is not bound to the assemblage making it up now, as this is forever vanishing downstream in the flow of exchange; in this respect it is different from its stuff and not the sum of it. We have thus the case of a substantial entity enjoying a sort of *freedom* with respect to its own substance, an independence from that same matter of which it nonetheless wholly consists. However, though independent of the sameness of this matter, it is dependent upon the change of it, on its progressing permanently and sufficiently, and there is no freedom in this. Thus the exercise of the freedom which the living thing enjoys is rather a stern *necessity*. The necessity we call "need," which obtains only where existence is unassured and identity a continual task. . . . The living individual exists at any time in one simultaneous composition of stuff, but is not identical with it—because it is, while coinciding with it, already in the act of passing beyond it.[6]

Even at this level of analysis, where plant and animal are as yet undistinguished and where motility and consciousness have not yet appeared on the horizon, certain features of the organism's mode of existence stand out as significant. In the first place, the organism is not a static substance whose identity is maintained by physical forces within itself. Its existence is less a state of affairs than a continuing performance of self-sustaining processes involving intercourse with what is not itself. The "self" of the organism is pitted against the "other" of the world, "within which, by which and against which it is committed to maintain itself."[7] The roots of what the philosophical anthropologists call man's "world-openness,"—his freedom with regard to a world on which he nonetheless depends—are found here. The metabolically maintained selfhood of the organism is the ontological base as well as the evolutionary source of the self-constitution of man in society.

Next, we note that the distinction between the identity of the organism and the physical sameness of its parts—its freedom with regard to its substance—makes it not less but more dependent on its environment. An inorganic thing cast into the emptiness of interstellar space might survive indefinitely, but a living being

6. *Ibid.*, 191.
7. *Ibid.*, 196.

would perish. The potential independence of the inorganic is the measure of its lack of freedom. It is only because it lacks any potential for self-realization and renewal that the inorganic thing can be free of the matter required for renewal. The polarity that life establishes between self and world involves the self in the necessary business of assuring its being in ways that affect the world:

> What, in its total effect, appears to be the maintaining of the given condition, is in fact achieved by way of a continuous moving beyond the given condition. There is an openness, a horizon, intrinsic to the very existence of the organic individual. Concerned with its being, engaged in the business of it, it must *for the sake* of this being let go of it as it is now so as to lay hold of it as it will be. Its continuation is always more than mere preservation. Organic individuality is achieved in the fact of otherness, as its own ever challenged goal, and is thus teleological. . . . Teleology comes in where the continuous identity of being is not assured by mere inertial persistence of substance, but is something continually executed by something *done,* and by something which *has* to be done in order to stay on at all.[8]

To call organic existence "teleological" means neither to credit the organism with an imagined consciousness of purpose nor to claim for its existence any purposes beyond itself. Organic existence is teleological in that the organism is oriented to its own survival; and this is not a state but a constant goal assured only by continuing, appropriate processes directed toward the otherness of the world. There is a sense in which conscious purpose in the anthropological sense may be considered as only a special case of this less-exalted phenomenon.

Every species interacts with its environment in its own way, and at the level of the organism as such we are still far from the specifically human mode of action described by Gehlen as "the transformation and interpretation of natural conditions by the application of intelligence."[9] Yet already the phenomenon of metabolism preconsciously embodies the imperative of transformative action. The substance of the world must be transformed, metabolized, to meet

8. *Ibid.,* 197.
9. Arnold Gehlen, "An Anthropological Model," *The Human Context,* I (1968–69), 11–20.

the requirements of the organism, but, no less significant, transformation has its limits and obeys its own necessities. Not only must
the organism find appropriate material to metabolize—that is, a
potentially habitable world—but the effects of its activity must
not so alter the environment that it ceases to be habitable. Sustaining itself by what amounts to interference with the environment,
the living being must maintain its supporting world, and though
the environment is altered by the activities of the self, the needs
that must be met are not. In other words, the requirements of the
organism are not products of the process through which they are
to be met. In the case of a cultural and historical being like man,
this observation requires qualification but the basic point holds.

Gehlen observes that: "It is only the re-shaping of nature as
it stands, of nature in the raw, that produces the sphere, in which
man can maintain himself . . . a 'second nature,' whose multiplicity is quite as endless as that of the first sphere but which has
passed through the hands, the intelligence and the phantasy of
man. In this activity, which extends from weapons, tools and techniques of living to the 'great houses,' the imaginary interpretations
of a meaning of the world, nothing is immanent, all is plastic and
mobile—it was for this reason that man was able to expand over
the whole of the globe in spite of the great variety of climatic, biological and geographical conditions encountered in its different environments."[10] The necessity of culture as the expression of man's
creativity is no less a sign of his special brand of finitude. To be a
cultural being means to be capable of genuine novelty in answering
the far-from-novel requirements of existence. Below mankind, novelty usually appears only when a new species enters the scene, but
in the human case novelty is not only compatible with specific
identity but even typical of it. Gehlen's remark that "all is plastic
and mobile" should not mislead us. Old problems provoke new
solutions, and in the course of history new, specifically cultural
requirements manifest themselves. The luxuries of one generation
can become the perceived needs of the next. But this does not mean
that the basic repertoire of human needs and abilities is altered.
Technical improvements in the management of the relationship
between man and world—even the emergence of a new level of

10. *Ibid.*, 16.

problems and solutions—do not mean that the requirements of the species no longer have to be met. At every level, the relationship between the living being and its environment is such that the active yet dependent partner is the one whose identity endures unchanged, for the transformation of substance that occurs in the encounter is at once an assault on the integrity of the environment and the necessary condition for the continuing identity of the organism. On the human level, this means that while man reforms the world within the limits of its causal nexus and in answer to his biologically and culturally given requirements, his action never touches the essence of his self. One's self is the individual, though culturally mediated, expression of the enduring identity of human nature, and this, like the nature of any other species, essentially requires the maintenance of a certain sort of world.

Gehlen himself noted that his concept of man as a world-transforming, self-constituting being, characterized not by static contemplation but by action, brings him close to the praxis-centered anthropology of Karl Marx. The difference is that Marx conceives history not so much as the expression of human nature but as its formative process. Gehlen does not underestimate the importance of history, but he relativizes it by relating it to certain constant requirements of the species:

> If we try to explain man's special position as a concomitant of his need to reshape nature, we are immediately reminded of the fact that, because he is so ill equipped to defend himself with "organic weapons," because his instincts have lost their acuteness and certainty and because his sensual acts, although diverse, are nonetheless modest, man is so structured as to qualify for the epithet once used by Herder, when he spoke of "deficient" being. Certainly, if man, with his inherent physique and with the unreliability of his instincts, were exposed to nature in the raw in the same way as animals, he could never survive; it is only his ability to change nature by the application of intelligence that saves him.[11]

Man's being is not open to the world merely in the organismic sense, for he, and he alone, must consciously fabricate a world appropriate to his constitutionally given needs. Between every other

11. *Ibid.*, 19.

animal and its world there is a balance maintained, where necessary, by instinctually directed behavior. Man, in contrast, must
both make and discover the world suitable to him. He makes it in
the sense that he creates the cultural forms, institutions, and symbols that stabilize his life in the absence of instinctual guidance.
He discovers it in his awareness that not every arrangement is
equally appropriate to him. This double process of creation and
discovery takes place in the span of human life, at once in the biographical span of the individual and in the historical duration of
the cultural community.

As with so many of the complexities of man's existence, the
truth about man's relationship to the world he occupies is most
readily expressed in the language of religious myth—in this case,
the myth of divinely willed cosmic order. According to this myth
in all its many forms, man has a certain place in the God-given
order of things. Sometimes this place is seen as a direct consequence of the original creative act; more usually, as modified by
subsequent human actions. Such acts have the éffect of bringing
man up against what will subsequently be the limits of his condition. Adam and Eve eat the fruit of the forbidden tree and are cast
into the world of mortality and labor. Gilgamesh journeys in search
of the fruit of youth regained but loses it almost as soon as it is
found. Everywhere, in the words of Aeschylus, man "suffers unto
truth," and the truth he must recognize is the fact of his finitude.
As Hans-Georg Gadamer points out:

> What a man has to learn through suffering is not this or that particu-
> lar thing, but the knowledge of the absoluteness of the barrier that
> separates him from the divine. It is ultimately a religious insight—
> the kind of insight that gave birth to Greek tragedy. Thus experience
> is experience of human finitude. The truly experienced man is one
> who knows that he is master neither of time nor of the future. . . .
> Experience teaches us to recognize reality. What is properly gained
> from all experience, then, is to know what is. But "what is," here,
> is not this or that thing, but "what cannot be done away with"
> —Ranke.[12]

12. Hans-Georg Gadamer, *Truth and Method*, trans. William Glen-Doepel (London, 1975), 230.

What cannot be done away with is the human condition as such. According to the myth of divine order, the peculiarity of this condition is that it allows man a considerable freedom that may or may not be positively used. Man is under an obligation to God and himself to become what intentionally he is in the divine scheme. Human action is necessary to the construction and maintenance of an order that expresses more than human will. At a certain level, the order of creation depends upon one of its constituent parts. Man can be seen as the steward of creation or, in Heidegger's evocative phrase, the shepherd of Being. If myth is, as Thomas Mann has it, "the garment of mystery," then the myth of divinely willed cosmic order and man's place within it garbs the mysteries of finite freedom and uncertain destiny that are constitutive of man's lot in life.

The unique beauty of the myth is that it not only describes a situation that we can independently recognize as our own but explains it as well. The ambiguity of the political condition, which is both the product and the precondition of human action, is attributed to events of supernatural significance that happened in the "once upon a time"—Eliade's *in illo tempore*—described by the myth. It is hardly surprising that the tale of the Fall of Man and the concomitant doctrine of Original Sin have played such an important part in Christian political thought from Saint Augustine to Joseph de Maistre, who refers to Original Sin as "explaining everything, and without which nothing can be explained." The mythic tale, whose events belong to a time before and constitutive of historical time, fills the puzzling cognitive gap that opens up whenever we ask not what we are but why. No criticism of any particular myth, nor even of mythical explanation as such, can do away with the puzzle that gave rise to the myth in the first place. Mythical explanation always takes the form of a dramatic tale that tells why things have become as they are. It is as such vulnerable to scientific and historical criticism that may find it incompatible with the state of knowledge arrived at independently. As Ricoeur in particular argues, this means that, while the symbolic truth of the myth may be acknowledged by modern scholarship, its pretension to provide an explanation for the world or any part of it will be rejected. The question then arises as to whether any alternative explanation of the political condition—one not vulnerable to the same criticism as the myth—is available.[13] This is where philosophical anthropology plays its most important part. Its explanation is necessarily less inclusive than that of myth, which, as we have seen, "explains everything." It is bound, as myth is not, by the discipline of philosophical discourse and by a body of scientific knowledge independent of itself. Instead of re-weaving the garment of mystery, philosophical anthropology aspires to discern the anatomy, the bodily structure, of man's world. It finds its resources in the sciences of nature, in historical and archeological scholarship, in the psychological and philosophical investigation of the life of consciousness, and in a critically adequate ontology.

Every man may be conceived as the intersection point of two orders, epistemologically distinct but ontologically one. Following traditional usage, let us call these the order of perception and the order of being. I do not merely stand at the crossing point able to choose which way I will go; I *am* that point, made what I am, on the one hand, by everything transient and enduring that coheres in the order of being and, on the other, by the peculiar historical and biographical circumstances in which I come to awareness of my place within it. The order in which I perceive things is not the order in which they come to be. I am aware of effects before I discover their causes. I encounter my mother and father before I learn of the generations who preceded them. I am always the center of the perceptual order but know that my being is only a fragment formed and de-formed in the unceasing flow of time. Each order has its radical—in the sense of fundamental—philosophical science. Phenomenology is the science of the order of perception, delineating the ways in which reality comes to be known in the life of man. Ontology is the science of the order of being, charting as best it can, within the limits of finite consciousness, the most universal features of what we may discover the world to be. Just as man is the meeting point of perception and being, so philosophical anthropology incorporates the insights of phenomenology and ontology.

13. Jack Lively (trans. and ed.), *The Works of Joseph de Maistre* (New York, 1965), 165; Paul Ricoeur, *The Symbolism of Evil*, trans. Emerson Buchanan (Boston, 1967).

But this is not all. I spoke of philosophical anthropology drawing
not only on the spheres of ontology and phenomenology but on
natural and historical sciences also. It must do this because the
ontology of human existence has to take account of the finite freedom of psyche and spirit, expressed in cultural creation and historical activity, and of the condition that man as a type of living
being encounters in the face of resistant nature. In an early formulation of his position, Gehlen speaks of his analysis as starting in
the given, concrete situation in which he finds himself,

> with these contingent determinations, living together with these
> others, under given, even rather artificial, conditions of life, in a state
> and a people, with such a profession and property and these skills,
> such a language and so forth. . . . This reflection is from the outset
> and in an unforced way historical, in that the conditions of life in
> which I find myself have developed already without any assistance.
> In that I find my existence to be dependent upon and related to
> countless historical conditions, the aggregate of which is called cul-
> ture, the question arises of the essence of man as a social being, char-
> acterizable in such and such a way, who can conduct his life only on
> the basis of a nature which has been transformed in certain definite
> directions and to whose essence as a human being definite facts such
> as family, state, tradition, work, technique and so on belong.[14]

The framework of culture into which man is born is, in every
case, a particular historical realization of possibilities bounded by
the ontological condition in which his species finds itself. The fact
that this condition is characterized by freedom from instinctive
and automatic responses means that the universal "natural" condition of man is to be a cultural being, creating for himself the
balance between self and world that is lacking at the merely organic level of his existence. Political order, according to this conception, is the necessary correlate of man's relative freedom from
the constraints of preconscious forces without and within. Being
the work of man—a part of human destiny but not a provision of
his biological inheritance—order is always vulnerable. Culture sig-
nals its limitations, in comparison with the preconscious domain

14. Cited by Rüdiger Bubner in *Modern German Philosophy*, trans. Eric Mat-
thews (Cambridge, 1981), 209–10.

of instinct, not only in the periodic crises of meaning in which, individually or collectively, all sense of intelligibility seems to vanish from experience—the nervous or civilizational breakdown that paralyzes activity by denying it any perceivable purpose—but in the imperfection of the fit between the demands of collective life and the aspirations of the individual. The order that man imposes on man bears witness to the same limits of nature and condition as the order he imposes on the world. That, in principle, is why political order, in its narrow sense of institutions embodying authority through the regulation of unequal power relations, is a necessary dimension of cultural life. Questions of domination among wolves or succession among bees, for example, are settled more or less brutally in ways determined by genetic inheritance and therefore favorable to the survival needs of the species. But when man faces equivalent problems of dominion and inheritance, he can settle them only by force, which lacks the instinctively directed restraint that we find in other intraspecific battles, or by recourse to the conscious order of political-legal institutions.

To understand the uniqueness of this situation—which is the very core of the political condition—let us return once more to the fundamentals of the organic existence from which man sprang and to which, in part, his mode of being still belongs. Every being in nature, whether organism or inorganic body, exists in a state of dynamic equilibrium or balance, but this state is not the same in the two cases. Whereas the equilibrium of an inanimate body, like a crystal, is maintained in a closed system characterized by a physical balance immanent in its structure, the organism is an open system. Its equilibrium may be described as fluid, dependent upon an input of elements external to itself. This concept of fluid equilibrium describes the form of identity that we have already seen to characterize the organism—identity not only compatible with but dependent on the continuous change of its matter in the intercourse of self and world.

The living being depends upon the maintenance of a balance between itself and its world, and this must be assured through processes that are, from the purely physical point of view, continuously altering both world and self. The relationship between organism and environment must therefore be self-regulating, so that intercourse not only serves the short-term survival needs of the organism but assures the continuation of the world that allows it to be. Organic activity must simultaneously transform and conserve. That is the condition of life, for every organism requires, as its necessary condition, the existence of a certain sort of world.

What, though, does it mean to talk of "world" in this sense, where the term signifies less the totality of what is than the structure necessary to the support of particular forms of life? Work by Jakob von Uexküll, one of the biologists who influenced Gehlen's thinking, throws considerable light on the relationship between the animal and what he called its surrounding world (Umwelt). Common sense, confirmed by the popular conception of a scientifically knowable, objective world, tends to assume that every animal, as an inhabitant of a shared planet, experiences the world as much the same sort of place. This view allows room for differences due to variations in environment, sensory acuteness, the size of the animal, and what may loosely be called its intelligence, but these amount to nothing more than a diversity of perspectives that could, in principle, be arranged on a scale of accuracy relative to the world as it is in itself—that is to say, a world of items and processes endowed with measurable properties that are what they are regardless of any act by which they may be apprehended.

The development of modern physics since Einstein and the work of the quantum physicists requires a considerable modification of this supposedly scientific world-view, but what I want to emphasize here is its failure to do justice to the extent of the interdependence between the species and its world. Von Uexküll argued that every animal experiences its surroundings in a way strictly related to the vital activities necessary to its survival. In one sense, the world is indeed one planet shared by a multiplicity of species— destroy it physically, and the world of every animal would disappear. That is the truth of common-sense objectivism, founded in the ontological dependence of all real being on the inorganic level. But in another sense every species constitutes its own surrounding world, with its own spatial dimensions and its own specific content. Everything that is, is potentially available to experience, but what appears in the world of a given animal depends less on its objective reality than on the physical, sensory, and mental structure of the creature. The objective reality of the world—the world as object of experience—is species-specific, not because any animal chooses how the world is to be (even man, in the last resort, does not do that, although now he may choose whether it is to be at all) but because to a given species there corresponds a particular world. What is experienced as "the world" is that selection of cosmically available possibilities that serves the needs, primarily the survival needs, of the animal. To use an example favored by von Uexküll, the world of the common tick (*Ixodes rhicinus*) is structured around the distinction between what smells of butyric acid and has a temperature of 37 degrees centigrade, on the one hand, and everything else, on the other. These are the features characterizing the mammals on whom the tick must live and feed, and their presence in the environment is enough to cause the tick to bite. Simple information, adequate to the needs of the animal, triggers the mechanism necessary to survival. If we consider the defining features of the tick's world, it becomes clear that the relationship between a species and its world is essential in a more-than-material sense. For if there were no common tick, there would be no world of the type that the tick inhabits.[15]

The tick constitutes the world appropriate to its survival, and every higher animal follows in its path. But it is essential to note that, while this observation causes us to qualify what we mean by the objective reality of the world through the recognition of the contribution made by the experiencing subject, it does not undermine the principle of objectivity itself. The point to be made is not a subjectivist one. The world is, in every case, what it is, regardless of what any subject chooses to make it or defines it as being. But what the world is includes the subject who has, as much as the object of his activity—whether metabolic, practical, or theoretical—a certain place within it. To use the language of metaphysics, man is, like every organism, a participant in being and not an observer standing on the outside looking in. The mistake of simple objectivism is not its claim that the world is, beyond decision, a certain sort of place, but its failure to take account of the fact that the objective reality of the world includes the reality of the event

15. Konrad Lorenz, *Behind the Mirror: A Search for a Natural History of Human Knowledge*, trans. Ronald Taylor (London, 1976), 53–55.

in which world is disclosed. In ignoring this, a purely objectivist picture of man will fail to register the whole historical dimension of human experience, for history is the specifically human mode of experience. Although not constitutive of the structure of reality in an ontological sense, history is the field in which every disclosure or discovery of the real occurs. It is not true, as some have thought, that "to be is to be perceived"—that is to confuse the order of being with the particular perspective represented by the order of perception, and to reverse the fundamental—because ontological—truth that consciousness, at least of a finite human variety, depends for its very existence on a pre-existing sequence of independent strata. What is, however, true is that nothing that is not in some fashion and at some historical moment experienced can be said to be part of man's world.

By virtue of its nature and place within reality, every self has its necessary corresponding world. To a particular being at a particular time and place, the world will appear a certain way, and the way it appears is intrinsically related to prevailing interests of the self. The world can only appear one way to the common tick. This is a function of the identity between its "interests" and its unvarying survival needs. Man, in contrast, is a historical being with complex interests and concerns. He perceives the world differently at different times, relative to the particular concerns dominant, individually and socially, at any specific moment.

These concerns are rooted in the general condition that we share as members of the human race, as well as in the particularity of events. We have already seen that, in contrast to the inanimate body, the organism is characterized by the openness of its system, but what is in question here is something that is qualitatively, ontologically distinct. The openness of the organism consists in its need and ability to renew and maintain itself by exchange with its environment. At the level of animal life, where it becomes reasonable to talk of "experience," this environment is experienced as a "surrounding world" (*Umwelt*) whose defining features are correlated to the needs of the animal. The relationship between animal and world is such that the former receives from the latter just the information most likely to be helpful for its survival. In the 1920s, Max Scheler noted that one of the distinguishing marks of human experience was its openness to biologically irrelevant and even harmful impressions. Later writers have drawn on Adolf Portmann's work on human fetal development to argue that man is a biologically "unfinished" animal who can be said to enter the world prematurely and who undergoes in the first year after birth essential developments which, in the case of other higher animals, have already taken place within the womb. At a crucial stage of his existence the human being is exposed to the stimuli of a world with which he is, in biological terms alone, utterly unfitted to cope. He is, in Gehlen's term, a constitutionally endangered species—a point that will be recognized by any parent who has had the worry of trying to protect a toddler from the harmful effects of his promiscuous curiosity.

Lacking instinctual guidance, it is from the family, as cultural community rather than as biological unit, that the child first learns what he must do as well as who he is. And the family itself, through the experience of each of its living members, has acquired from the wider historical community of which it is part the lessons that it transmits. The instinctual deficiency of the human child is compensated by the cultural inheritance in which he comes to share. The apparently effortless acquisition of identity and language presents the child with a world already interpreted by his fellows and a place already made within it. Although he may later reject both, this is the point of contingency from which the child starts and whose marks he will bear until the day of his death. Seeming to be the passive recipient of cultural tradition, the child is living the individual human destiny through the active constitution of his mature—that is, culturally informed—self. In Gadamer's words, "we stand always within tradition, and this is no objectifying process, *i.e.* we do not conceive of what tradition says as something other, something alien. It is always part of us, a model or exemplar, a recognition of ourselves which our later historical judgement would hardly see as a kind of knowledge, but as the simplest preservation of tradition."[16]

This does not imply that there are not ways in which consciousness is impelled by what Scheler called the vital drives belonging

16. Gadamer, *Truth and Method*, 259.

to our specific organic constitution; but not only are these resist-
ible—man may even take his own life—they also permit an enormous variety of response, as is apparent in, for instance, the range
of human approaches toward food and sexuality. Thus even our organic needs are brought to consciousness in a cultured form, and
are experienced both as preconscious drives and as habitualized
desires possessing and even provoked by cultural models such as
recipe books and pornography. If we remember Hartmann's words
that while individual consciousness divides, the spiritual world of
culture unites, and note too the fragility of every culture as an order maintained by conscious acts lacking instinctive regulation,
if, finally, we recall the dependence of every living being upon the
maintained stability of the world, we will understand why the order that man imposes on the world—from which, nonetheless, it
seems mysteriously to derive—requires as its supplement and last
resort the order of power that he imposes on himself and his
fellows.

Power among men may simply mean possession of overwhelming force, but as Plessner notes,

> it can be different. It then represents a decision making power which,
> no matter how acquired, must be circumscribed and defined. A defi-
> nition of power also defines rights, and is based upon rights, no mat-
> ter what the nature of these rights may be, whether they be those
> traditionally safeguarded by common law, by sacred custom, or
> established by statute law. This is true also whatever the scope of
> power, since even unlimited powers have to be described and de-
> fined. Human power then is not identical with might, and must be
> differentiated from it. Might is transformed within the framework of
> a legal system which, in turn, depends upon it. Human power is by
> necessity linked to right. Power and right belong together structur-
> ally even though frequently one appears as a counter-weight to the
> other: right as a check and restraint, power as exploding anomic en-
> ergy. The processes of acquiring and wielding power yield to given
> regulations only conditionally and by nature embody the danger that
> threatened to disturb or destroy order.[17]

17. Helmuth Plessner, "The Emancipation of Power," *Social Research*, XXXI
(1964), 155–56.

The formation of institutions integrates the order of power with the order of meaning. Power without law or custom is experienced as a meaningless threat to life. Naked might possesses no authority. It may force everything except the gates of the mind, which only the key of meaning can open. Belonging purely to the level of organic life, might in the sense of mere physical force is foreign to the spiritual world of cultural meaning. Being able to give no account of itself, it cannot be legitimate. Yet might is always present, not making right, but forming with it the poles between which the political order is strung. Might and right together, integrated more or less uneasily in institutional order, structure the political condition as surely as the hive is projected in the genes of the bees who live and die within it.

FOUR

THE LIMITS OF ANTHROPOLOGY AND THE ANTHROPOLOGICAL HORIZON

At this point we must pause to ask what our inquiry thus far has established, for there is a sense in which the arguments developed consistently through the opening chapters come to a dead end with the conclusion of chapter 3. We have run up against the limits of a certain line of argument and, if the inquiry is to get any further, we must ask what these limits signify, what indeed they are, and whether there is any way of getting beyond them. Are the limits absolute, barring the way to further philosophical exploration? Or do they mark merely a horizon imposed by the limits of the point from which we started—man's place within nature?

Careful attention to the peculiarities of man's relationship to nature has allowed us to argue to the point at which the necessity of political activity and of institutional order can be established. Starting from positions developed in the early sections of Max Scheler's essay *Die Stellung des Menschen im Kosmos*—precisely those concerned with "Man's Place in Nature," as the title of the English translation misleadingly calls the whole work—we have developed a perspective upon the political-cultural realm that enables us to see politics as a permanent and vital necessity in the life of a species lacking in instinctual guidance and in genetically given answers to the questions thrown up in the struggle for existence. In large part we have restated in outline a theory of the human condition that was first thought through by a number of Scheler's younger contemporaries. In its turn, Nicolai Hartmann's ontology provided this theory with an adequate philosophical foundation, permitting us to grasp the essence of man's finite freedom as he experiences it in his relationship to the other beings of the world.

Nothing of this is now to be abandoned. Rather, we must ask whether what we have so far is anything more than a partial perspective—an essay in philosophical anthropology that is, in a sense, merely a prelude to the examination of political order. The inquiry must turn back upon itself and back to Scheler, not in order to undermine what has been established already but to overcome the limits of what alone is now in focus. It seems to me that these limits are of two rather different kinds. In the first place, the anthropological position developed in the first three chapters fails to take account of an essential dimension of political activity— the sense in which man's endeavors to construct a human-satisfying order involve more than simply the creation of institutional shelters against the perils of life. Central to man's ordering of his own existence is the quest to attune the order he constructs to an order he senses as in some way inherent in the universe that he did not create but which, perforce, he must inhabit. Political order must not merely *be*, it must be right; and right, in this context, means in as exact accord as possible with the order of being as a whole. In the second place, while the argument of previous chapters establishes the necessity of political activity and institutions, it says nothing about how these are to be directed and oriented. Brute necessity, born out of natural insufficiencies, gives us no conception of what is involved in political judgment and only the barest outlines for an understanding of political motivation.

Turning back upon itself, our inquiry leads us back to Scheler and to that summation of his ideas on philosophical anthropology that appeared in Germany shortly before his death in 1928 under the title *Die Stellung des Menschen im Kosmos.* When in 1958 the Beacon Press announced the forthcoming publication of Hans Meyerhoff's translation of *Die Stellung*, the book was to be called *The Place of Man in the Universe*, but by the time it appeared in 1961 it had become *Man's Place in Nature*. The change was of more than bibliographical significance. It reflected Meyerhoff's one-sidedly naturalistic approach to Scheler's thought and his dismissal of the importance of Scheler's discussion of *Geist* or Spirit as of no

more than biographical importance. Since Scheler, here as elsewhere, argued that it was precisely man's spiritual capacity that set
him apart from all merely natural beings, the change in title was
seriously misleading. The philosophical anthropology that Scheler
sought to develop and which only his death prevented him from
bringing to fruition in anything more than fragmentary form involved much more than a descriptive analysis of man's position
within the natural world. In the preface to *Die Stellung*, Scheler
remarked that "the questions 'What is man?' and 'What is man's
place in the nature of things?' have occupied me more deeply than
any other philosophical question since the first awakening of my
philosophical consciousness."[1] Scheler always insisted that there
could be no answer to these questions that did not take full account of man's status as a particular type of natural being, but,
no less significant for his anthropology, he argued that any answer
that stopped at this point would necessarily fail to grasp the essential truth about human nature and about the universe in which
man found himself. "Man's place in nature" is an aspect of his position in the cosmos as a whole, but it is not the whole of it nor
even its most significant part. Rather, Scheler maintained, the
uniqueness of man's relationship to the world of nature is only
the necessary precondition for the effectiveness of spiritual being
within the process of the whole.

Spirit does not originate with man, but only in and through him
can it become an effective and ultimately, if man attends to its requirements, the *most* effective factor in the unfolding drama of the
real. Spirit enters reality in man, who alone has a consciousness
capable of grasping it. Knowledge of spirit is not a variety of nor
a development from the forms of awareness characteristic of even
the highest forms of animal life. Man possesses these forms of
awareness as well—possesses them indeed to the highest degree.
All "practical" knowledge leading to a more effective control of the
environment is merely an extension of the form of consciousness
that we find already in animals. "Between the clever chimpanzee
and an Edison, taking the latter only as a technician, there is only
a difference in degree—though a great one to be sure."[2] But the

1. Max Scheler, *Man's Place in Nature*, trans. Hans Meyerhoff (Boston, 1961), 3.
2. *Ibid.*, 36.

human technician is always more than that, for beside practical intelligence and what Scheler calls "knowledge for control," man seeks to know and can know things in themselves. Knowledge of spirit is only possible for a being who can, as it were, stand back from the business of life to attend in love and awe to the essence of things. It is knowledge of spirit, possible only to man, and not a sophisticated variety of practical animal consciousness that constitutes the basic, metaphysical distinctiveness of the human species. It is the emergence of spirit in man that means that man's nature and condition are not merely to be another organism within nature but to be the point in being in and through which the metaphysical fate of the whole is decided.

I use the term *metaphysical* advisedly, for Scheler's philosophical anthropology cannot be properly understood without reference to the metaphysics of the interpenetration of *Geist* (spirit) and *Drang* (drive or *élan vital*) that characterizes his ultimate view of the world. Like the *Philosophische Anthropologie*, Scheler's *Metaphysik* was left unwritten at his death, but there is enough in his late writings to enable us to see the direction that both books would have taken and to understand the extent to which the one implied the other. If, as the *Philosophische Anthropologie* would have argued, the essence of man were not to be found in his spiritual capacity, through which spirit becomes effective in the world, the interpenetration of *Geist* and *Drang*—the guiding theme of the *Metaphysik*—could not occur. Scheler does not, like Hartmann, set man in the context of the world-order characterized by certain structural relations that can be known through ontological analysis, but rather locates man in a metaphysical history of the becoming of God in the world through the spiritualization—Scheler sometimes says deification—of one who is already an actor on the world stage. For Scheler, the spiritual aspect of man is nothing less than the opportunity for the realization of God.

Some readers will be impatient of such formulations. Many more will wonder what positive contributions they make to an inquiry into political order. Certainly, if we take it seriously, Scheler's metaphysical argument will call into question not the value of the sort of philosophical anthropological analysis carried out in earlier chapters but any claim that it might make to provide an integral and adequate understanding of the political condition in which

man necessarily exists. Hans Meyerhoff's mistranslation has
served us well up to this point. The reduction of "the place of man
in the cosmos" to "man's place in nature" has enabled us to understand the necessity of politics in the economy of human existence
and so to undermine the pretension to truth of all those ideologies
that promise us a postpolitical future without institutional guidance and constraint. But, as I have also suggested, the view that
emerged, though accurate so far as it goes, is a limited one whose
limitations appear at just the point where, having understood the
necessity of consciously guided political action, we ask how consciousness itself is to find guidance. It may be that Scheler's metaphysics is, in the last resort, untenable, but the desire to achieve a
clear and unambiguous anthropology of politics in terms of man's
place in nature cannot alter the fact that the range of his inquiry
and the breadth of his anthropology, in comparison with that of
some of his successors, allow us to open up areas of questioning
before which the narrower paths peter out.

    Let me illustrate this by looking at a work in which the possibili-
ties of anthropological inquiry through the exploration of man's
place in nature are achieved to the highest degree. Arnold Gehlen's
Der Mensch, seine Natur und seine Stellung in der Welt (Man, his
nature and place in the world) was first published in 1940. By 1966
it had run through eight editions in Germany. Writing nearly thirty
years after its publication, Gehlen admitted that "many parts of the
book had undoubtedly dated or even been wrongly conceived in the
first place." "But," he continued, "the book's remarkable longevity
points to the existence of a problem, for it would seem that it still
gratifies a persistent need, the need presumably to possess a model
conception, which was not at variance either with modern man's
inner experiences or with the real life experiences which he has
undergone over recent turbulent decades and which also made it
possible for him to organise, at least within limits, his ever-grow-
ing store of disjointed knowledge."[3]

    In the same essay, Gehlen describes Scheler's *Die Stellung* as
having "opened a door, which could not be passed by." For Gehlen,

    3. Arnold Gehlen, "An Anthropological Model," *The Human Context*, I (1968–
69), 11–20.

as for Scheler, the anthropological question, What is Man? was *the* pressing philosophical issue into which all others had been resolved. He shared the view expressed variously by Scheler, by Heidegger, and, as we shall see, by Voegelin that at a time when man had accumulated an unprecedented stock of scientific knowledge through the momentous development of both the natural and the human sciences his knowledge of himself was more obscure than ever before. As Heidegger has put it, "No epoch has accumulated so great and so varied a store of knowledge concerning man as the present one. No other epoch has succeeded in presenting its knowledge of man so forcibly and so captivatingly as ours, and no other has succeeded in making this knowledge so quickly and so easily accessible. But also, no epoch is less sure of its knowledge of what man is than the present one. In no other epoch has man appeared so mysterious as in ours."[4]

The crisis of human self-interpretation explored in Scheler's late essays was the starting point for all the writers mentioned above. While Heidegger and Voegelin pursued lines of inquiry that involved a decisive break with the anthropological perspective— Heidegger toward what he called "fundamental ontology" and Voegelin toward a philosophy of order and history—Gehlen attempted to reform philosophical anthropology from within. As Gehlen saw it, Scheler had opened the right door but had left the doorway cluttered with the detritus of an outdated metaphysical dualism signaled by his identification of the human essence in terms of "spirit." Although many of Scheler's insights were taken up and developed in a most fruitful way in Gehlen's work, it is important to recognize that what Gehlen rejected was just what the older thinker had considered most vital.

The significance of this rejection is our immediate concern; later we shall examine Voegelin's diametrically opposed response to Scheler's anthropology. The contrast is instructive, for, as we shall see, the very elements of *Die Stellung* that Gehlen excised from the anthropology he presents in *Der Mensch* were those that provided the starting point for Voegelin's inquiry. What Scheler sought to hold together, his successors developed apart. Against a political

4. Martin Heidegger, *Kant and the Problem of Metaphysics*, trans. James S. Churchill (Bloomington, Ind., 1962), 216.

background dominated by the rise of the Third Reich, in which the question of the essence of man became a matter of life or death for millions, the paths diverge, with serious practical as well as theoretical consequences. As they do so, it may seem that we are losing the range of vision, encompassing everything from the biological to the eschatological, which is one of the most striking things about Scheler's work. But the answer is not to fall back upon Scheler's own formulations. The paths in question—Gehlen's as well as Voegelin's—are paths forward. New insights are achieved, and new problems are brought into focus within a more clearly defined horizon. We must follow each path in turn, and only when we have reached the end of each can we ask whether there is still a common ground in view.

It is in this spirit that we approach the question of the limitations of the perspective adopted in *Der Mensch*. The limits of Gehlen's anthropology, like the limits of Hartmann's ontology (which will concern us later), are such that they are not only instructive in themselves, but the very partiality of the picture that emerges within them can provide us with a true part of the broader view of existence that we are seeking. It may even be that only the narrowing of vision that we note in the passage from Scheler's anthropology to Gehlen's allows us to bring to light certain issues of political order that are left aside in other post-Schelerian developments. That expectation, which has still to be justified, was the working assumption behind our opening chapters. Its value will only be tested when, in the third part of the book, we employ the insights found along both paths to provide an analysis of the particular problems of political order in the modern world. There, the achievements of one line of inquiry will help us fill in the gaps left by another; and, while there can be no question of a wholesale synthesis between the traditions variously represented by Gehlen and Voegelin, the tension between the two will prove to be one of complementarity more than of contradiction.

Having said this, let us return to Gehlen and his first great book. The aim behind it was encapsulated in its title. *Man, His Nature and Place in the World* was intended to provide a descriptive analysis of the human condition that took full account of the findings of both the biological and the human sciences as well as of the philosophical analyses of consciousness associated with the school of phenomenology. Gehlen had read and been impressed by Hartmann's *Zur Grundlegung der Ontologie* (On the foundations of ontology), which was published in 1935, but he felt that Hartmann's hopes of achieving a systematic, philosophically adequate understanding of reality as a whole—Hartmann's cherished lifelong ambition—was doomed to failure. As Gehlen later wrote, "under no circumstances might a philosophical system lose contact with the sciences, and the structure of the sciences was then being daily extended in all its dimensions, so that it was no longer possible to form a comprehensive view of the whole field from any one vantage point."[5] The turn from epistemology and ontology to philosophical anthropology, which Heidegger had noted as typical of contemporary German thought in his 1929 study of Kant, represented a turn from a philosophy centered on the question of Being as a whole toward one centered on Man. Despair at the possibility of ever achieving an understanding of a universe whose structure seemed more mysterious each year was matched by the hope that scientific knowledge of the cultural and biological conditions of human existence would provide an alternative starting point for philosophical inquiry. In his own work, Heidegger called into question not only the philosophical credentials of such an anthropology but also the forms of thought to which it was in part a reaction. At the same time, he remained the most sympathetic and perceptive critic of the philosophical anthropological approach. In the sections of *Kant and the Problem of Metaphysics*, a book dedicated to the memory of Scheler in which he discusses the Schelerian enterprise, Heidegger noted that "anthropology today . . . is not only the name of a discipline; the term denotes a fundamental tendency characteristic of the present position of man with regard to himself and to the totality of the essent. According to this tendency, a thing is known and understood only when it receives an anthropological explanation. Today, anthropology not only seeks the truth concerning man but also claims to have the power of deciding the meaning of truth as such."[6]

5. Gehlen, "An Anthropological Model," 11.
6. Heidegger, *Kant and the Problem of Metaphysics*, 216.

Although this final sentence is not really true of Scheler himself, it certainly anticipates the position taken consistently by Gehlen in *Der Mensch*. Gehlen could utilize aspects of a structural ontology such as Hartmann's without adopting Hartmann's own ontological criteria of philosophical truth, because, as he saw it, the new ontology provided an analysis of the real precisely as seen from the perspective of man conceived as a certain type of natural being inhabiting and acting effectively upon a world that possessed certain knowable characteristics. Ontology, in the work of Gehlen, becomes, quite consciously, a supplement to anthropology, rather than, as in Hartmann, its necessary foundation. As it does so, the measure of truth is shifted from objective knowledge of the structure of the world to the subjective demands of man as a being engaged in the struggle for existence. Thus, while employing the categories of an ontology that conceives reality in terms of a complex of interpenetrating but analytically distinct strata, Gehlen renews the tradition of what was then called "organic philosophy" or *Lebensphilosophie*, associated with Hans Driesch and more recently with the cultural criticism of Konrad Lorenz. In this tradition, the test of truth in human thought and action is identified with its utility in the struggle for survival. No higher measure of truth is admitted, and therefore the ultimate standard of what is right or wrong in human affairs becomes the question of biological fitness.

Lorenz himself has recently given a brief and typically pithy illustration of this approach in *Civilized Man's Eight Deadly Sins*, but Gehlen's work still remains its most sophisticated and carefully formulated application in the field of the human sciences. Let us be clear about one thing: the viewpoint that Gehlen adopts is not a variety of what is normally called biological determinism. It does not, like the arguments of the sociobiologists, depend upon an ultimate explanation of social life and political institutions as being effects of pregiven genetic patterns. Gehlen learned well the lessons of Hartmann's ontology, and he accepted that there are no unbroken causal chains that run across the ontological barrier between the stratum of organic nature and those of human consciousness and culture. What has been called Gehlen's "perfected biological approach" recognizes the sphere of nature as the necessary precondition for human existence but not, except in the tasks it sets him, the formative influence upon man's achievements. In Gehlen's view, it is not what David Barash has called the "whispering within"—the presence of genetically structured behavioral patterns—that dictates the form of human institutions, but their absence that makes the formation of institutions necessary.[7]

Gehlen's approach to the understanding of the human condition is what we might call the pure anthropological perspective, unsullied by any lingering presence of what he calls the "other worldly" metaphysic of spirit incarnate. Man is not to be understood, as Scheler supposed, as the point of entry of world-transcendent spirit into the drama of the real. But no more can he be understood as merely another animal interacting with a pregiven environment. Rejecting Scheler's doctrine of spirit, Gehlen retains two other crucial features of Schelerian anthropology—the understanding of human existence by means of comparison with the existence of other animals, and the designation of man as a uniquely "world-open" being. The two are connected, for the discovery of man's world-openness occurs as a result of the contrast that emerges when human and animal existence are set alongside each other. Scheler had noted that by every criterion of natural science the comparison of human with "animal" existence is well-nigh worthless; for, in natural scientific terms alone, man has infinitely more in common with his nearest animal relatives than they have with the lower forms of animal life. Gehlen also expresses his reservations about the feasibility of making "anything more than trivial statements about 'the animal' as an abstract phenomenon," but, like Scheler, he points to the benefits of adopting what is admittedly an apparently scientifically dubious comparison for the purposes of anthropological inquiry.

This is how Gehlen later summed up the advantages of the comparative approach:

> The special position enjoyed by man in the realm of nature, which is an obvious fact, was not at all obvious when, in accordance with the theory of evolution, one assumed a straight-forward development

7. Konrad Lorenz, *Civilized Man's Eight Deadly Sins*, trans. Marjorie Latzke (London, 1974); David Barash, *The Whispering Within: Evolution and the Origin of Human Nature* (New York, 1979). For a measured criticism of sociobiology, see Roger Trigg, *The Shaping of Man: Philosophical Aspects of Sociobiology* (Oxford, 1982).

from the anthropoids to man. But if one proceeded in the opposite direction and placed man in relief against the background of animal reality, then his special position was evident from the outset, which made it possible to add a rider to the evolutionary hypothesis, establishing a particular kind of natural constitution for man similar to that which has actually been observed within the sphere of "retardation." But above all it was possible to describe man *indirectly*, namely, both in comparison with, and in contradistinction to, "the animal." This is an extremely important point; for at no time has man been able to understand himself other than in an indirect manner, be it in his relationship to Gods and Demons, i.e. to super-men, from whom he was able to distinguish himself by relating himself to them, or in his relationship to the natural world, with which he was able to identify, only to break down the equation again—just like Cartesian man: an angel who lives in a machine. Since Darwin, on the other hand, man has evolved from animal predecessors, although this process of evolution has been both continuous and desultory at one and the same time and the concept of "evolution" has had to cover both its similarity and its dissimilarity. The ultimate reason why all definitions of man are necessarily indirect is no doubt that man exists only within the bounds of his relationship to the "extra-human," only as a being that, by going outside itself both in thought and deed, by identifying itself with "the other," finds itself again—a relationship which is difficult to grasp in logical terms, which Hegel tried to master with his dialectics and G. H. Mead with his concept of "taking the role of the other," and which has been mastered today, albeit in a somewhat simplified form, by the cybernetic formula, which speaks of feed-back systems. Although Scheler, who remained caught up in an abstract dualism, certainly did not progress this far, by describing man in contradistinction to the animal he nonetheless put more into his system than he knew how to get out of it.[8]

Gehlen assumes from the outset that the great virtue of the descriptive and comparative approach is the opportunity it affords for understanding man in contradistinction to "the animal." As Landgrebe puts it, he "takes as the guiding principle of his thesis the supposition that man must not be understood with a view to what he has in common with animals, and some subsequently super-

8. Gehlen, "An Anthropological Model," 15.

added factor, but that all the factors which are efficaciously active in man, beginning with the lowest, purely organic ones, must from the outset be grasped in their specific significance."[9] Man's essence, if we may use the term, is to be found in his own specific mode of existence. Seen in this light, man is not one among the animals, not even one to whom a higher, metaphysically distinct element of soul or spirit has been added. He is a quite unique type of being whose relationship to the world on which his survival depends is utterly different from that subsisting between the animal and its environment. The specific difference of man is a difference not of degree but of kind, and no feature of man's being can be understood in its actual operations unless it is comprehended as a particular functional part in a whole unique structure of existence. Even the organic processes and cognitive operations common to man and animal alike are misunderstood unless, in the human case, they are conceived as elements within a quite distinct form of life.

Thus, while he rejects Scheler's identification of man's specific difference with his endowment with spirit, Gehlen, on the surface at least, is quite as committed to the view that what is in question in anthropology is a being essentially different from the animal. Under the influence of Darwinian evolutionism, naturalistic anthropologists tend to minimize the differences between human and animal life. Against this tendency, Gehlen insists that the equation of man and animal is precisely what prevents us from achieving a biological understanding of what is specifically human. The biology to which he appeals is what he calls "anthropobiology"—that is, an analysis of man's organic processes in terms of the functions they fulfill or fail to fulfill in the context of the specific totality of human existence, a form of life that not only could not be derived from the possibilities of animal existence but which the imperative preconditions of animal survival would seem to make impossible.

There is an analogy between Gehlen's approach and that of the Gestalt psychologists.[10] Like them, Gehlen argues that we have to grasp man's life experience as a unitary whole. Gestalt psycholo-

9. Ludwig Landgrebe, *Major Problems in Contemporary European Philosophy,* trans. Kurt F. Reinhardt (New York, 1966), 22.
10. See, in particular, the works of Max Wertheimer, Kurt Koffka, and Wolfgang Kohler.

gists reject the behaviorist approach, according to which human experience is made up of a succession of analytically distinct sensations. The Gestalt theorists point to the way in which the central nervous system in animals possessing consciousness as well as in man apprehends the world as an already constituted whole, a *Gestalt*, of an identifiable type. A psychology of the behaviorist type that seeks to understand experience as a combination of separate parts misses the point that it is only as elements within a subjectively integrated picture that the parts—the isolated, measurable sensations—appear at all. The sensations to which the behaviorists make exclusive appeal are real enough, but they enter the reality of human or animal experience as elements of an integral view of the world constituted by the central nervous system of the experiencing subject. Whatever light behaviorism may throw on the sources of particular experiences, it cannot explain experience as such, for what is experienced has already become a part of an organized whole.

The *Gestalt* that concerns Gehlen is the unique totality of the human form of life. Like the Gestalt psychologists, he does not deny the scientific credentials of evolutionary theory. What he does reject is the belief that what is essentially a genetic theory— a theory explaining the origins of particular identifiable life forms—can grasp the essential character of what actually exists in already constituted form. A theory of origins is not a morphology. What actually exists must be analyzed as a totality in which the analytically separable elements stand as functional parts to a whole capable of maintaining itself in the world. Seen in this light, human existence is an utterly distinct life form. While animal life is characterized by the adaptation of the species to a pre-existing environment, in man both organic adaptation and fixed environment are notable by their absence. As we have noted in earlier chapters, Gehlen observes that, in comparison with nonhuman animals, man is an underprivileged or deficient being that lacks both instinctual guidance and the sort of bodily equipment that would enable him to assure his survival. It is this very lack of adaptation that is man's mark of distinction. If such a being is to survive at all, he must adapt or transform the world in which he finds himself. As Landgrebe summarizes the argument:

All human functions, such as sensation, feeling, perception, language, derive from this their specific meaning, a meaning and significance which can in no way be compared with the role they play in animal life. These functions are not a simple actualization of a prior adaptation to a given environment. . . . They are functions on which a living being which does not enjoy, in an originary manner, a firm correlation of environment and organic functions, must of necessity depend. They must therefore be understood as the "self-activated performance by virtue of which man transforms the privative existential conditions of an underprivileged being into the chances of his survival." Man, by virtue of his nature, must of necessity be an active being, and the quintessence and sum total of that nature which he transforms by his action into that which serves life, is the world of culture and civilization. But in order to be able to act, man stands in need not only of a vista of possibilities but, in addition, of an actual independence of direct impulses; in short, the satisfaction of his needs and wants must be inhibited to some extent rather than being immediately fulfilled. Whereas in the animal sensation and reaction are directly interrelated, man owns the possibility of traversing the world in non-compulsive sensations (*triebfreien Empfindungen*) and of thus gaining a perspective of possibilities of "world over man." It is this capability of "retaining and restraining impulses" which brings to light man's "inwardness." All the sensorimotorial performances are not only carried out mechanically but with a self-awareness which moves them into the realm of cognition and makes them subject to control. Man must become conscious of himself in order to be able to survive as a human being. "He must acquire knowledge in order to become active; he must be active in order to stay alive tomorrow."[11]

In an essay "Man and History," first published in 1926, Scheler argued that the construction of a philosophical anthropology was the most urgent philosophical task for the age. By "philosophical anthropology" he means "a basic science which investigates the *essence* and *essential constitution* of man, his relationship to the realms of nature (organic, plant, and animal life) as well as to the source of all things, man's metaphysical origin as well as his physi-

11. Landgrebe, *Major Problems in Contemporary European Philosophy*, 23.

cal, psychic, and spiritual origins in the world, the forces and powers which move man and which he moves, the fundamental trends
and laws of his biological, psychic, cultural and social evolution,
along with their essential capabilities and realities."[12] By looking
at Gehlen's attainment in the context of Scheler's project we can
identify the significant limitations of what I have called the pure
anthropological approach of Der Mensch.

Prefiguring the already cited words of Heidegger, Scheler remarks that at no time have views concerning the "essence and origin of man" been more varied and less sure than in our own. "In
approximately ten centuries of history, this is the first in which
man finds himself completely and utterly 'problematical,' in which
he no longer knows what he is and simultaneously knows that he
does not have the answer." In the light of present knowledge, we
must look anew at "the being, called man, with an extreme and
methodical objectivity, and wonder." But this, Scheler admits, is
very difficult, because there is no problem more cluttered by the
presence of unacknowledged and unconsciously held assumptions
than the question of human nature. Scheler distinguishes five separate "fundamental ideas" of man that exert an influence among his
contemporaries. Each presents a distinct anthropological image
from whose assumptions fundamentally different ideas of the nature, structure, and origin of man derive. "For whether or not the
historian, sociologist, or philosopher of history is conscious and
aware of it, each historical doctrine is based on a particular kind of
anthropology."[13]

The five "fundamental ideas" are: the Christian doctrine of man
as a divinely created but fallen and sinful being; the Greek view of
man as a uniquely rational being; the naturalistic anthropology
that sees man as essentially homo faber—the maker and trans-
former of the world; the view that Scheler calls "pan-romantic" or
"Dionysian" and associates above all with the then-influential
views of Ludwig Klages, according to which man is a defective
product of evolution—"a complete deserter from life"—radically
alienated from nature by the very "spirit" or "mind" in which he

12. In Max Scheler, Philosophical Perspectives, trans. Oscar A. Haac (Boston,
1958), 65.
13. Ibid., 65, 69.

takes such pride; and, finally, what Scheler calls the "postulating atheism of seriousness and responsibility," most rigorously represented in Hartmann's *Ethik*, which pictures man as the uniquely purposeful inhabitant of an otherwise mechanistic universe.

For the moment, only the third and fourth positions concern us, for the anthropology of *Der Mensch* is a synthesis between the image of man-the-maker and the pessimistic naturalism or vitalism of the Dionysian view. It is worth quoting the paragraph in which Scheler identifies the root suppositions of the latter in order to bring out how fully they enter into the premises of Gehlen's rather original anthropology. Theodor Lessing, whom Scheler calls the "adroit publicist of this idea," encapsulated the theory in the formula "man is a species of predatory ape that gradually went mad with pride over its so-called 'mind.'" Scheler continues his examination of this line of thinking but notes that

> the Dutch anatomist Louis Bolk . . . more appropriately summed up the results of his investigation in this sentence: "Man is an infantile ape with deranged secretions." In a similar way, the Berlin physician Paul Alsberg claims to have discovered a "principle of humanity," not concerned with morphological comparison, in the "principle of degenerating organic functions." Strongly influenced by Schopenhauer, the argument runs like this: Man stands quite defenseless in his environment, altogether far less adapted to it than his closest animal relatives. Unable to further develop his organic functions, man has, therefore, developed a tendency to use as few organic functions as possible and to replace them by tools (language and conceptualization are judged to be "immaterial tools") which make it unnecessary to develop and sharpen the sensory organs. According to this theory, intelligence is not an *a priori* spiritual power requiring this disuse and making it possible, but, rather, the result of the fundamental refusal to use these organic functions, indeed, one of the modes of Schopenhauer's "negation of life by the will."[14]

Typically, as in the work of Klages, this line of thought places the principle of "spirit" in radical opposition to the "life force." In this way, the spirit/life dualism, which we also find in Scheler's

14. *Ibid.*, 83.

metaphysics, is reformulated as a principle of contradiction that cuts across the very form of human existence. While Scheler looked forward to an ever-increasing spiritualization of life, Klages taught that only a reawakening of the indwelling impulses of nature could save mankind from the spiritually induced atrophy of the life force. This idea became a major component in the anthropology of National Socialism with its persistent appeal to a renewed unity of "blood and soil," the recurrent symbols evoking, respectively, the inner and outer aspects of a single principle of life whose political expression would be the biologically based racial community.

Gehlen's argument precludes such a simplistic position. By adhering with exemplary rigor to the consequences of regarding man in a naturalistic light as an organically deficient being, he rules out the possibility of falling back upon the urges of the life force as a solution to the problems of existence. At the same time, his anthropology remains significantly bound by the limits of the Dionysian premise. In a roundabout way, he confirms the practical implications of Klages' cult of life even while denying the possibility of the answer that Klages himself gives. From the natural deficiencies of man, Gehlen deduces not the dualistic opposition of life and spirit but the necessity of a consciously formed cultural order. Human consciousness and the order of culture that derives from it are anthropological necessities. Consciousness is "the auxiliary means of the organic process,"[15] which is otherwise incurably defective. We cannot fall back upon what is no longer present in the human constitution. In place of the absent order of instinctual regulation, man must regulate his life by creating institutions. Lacking the natural endowment that would assure survival, he must equip himself with tools and weapons such as only conscious intelligence could devise.

A certain separation from nature is man's fate, for only in standing back from his immediate environment can he perceive it as an open field of objectively estimable possibilities. This, in turn, is the precondition for the transformative action on which human survival depends. Unable to adapt himself to the environment,

15. Ludwig Landgrebe, *Main Problems in Contemporary European Philosophy: From Dilthey to Heidegger*, trans. Kurt F. Reinhardt (New York, 1966), 23.

man must adapt it to him. Objectification of the environment, a function of human consciousness, permits the achievement of a humanly possible world of culture, and culture is the only nature in which man can survive.

Thus, starting from premises identical with Klages and the "Back to Nature" school, Gehlen arrives at the position he was later to formulate in the anti-Rousseauistic slogan "Back to Culture." The contrast here is apparent, but when we ask what is its significance the difference begins to disappear. The institutionalized world of culture is, as Gehlen describes it, a product of self-conscious, intelligent, transformative activity. In this sense it stands opposed to the human impossibility of raw nature—the vitalistic utopia of "blood and soil." But culture is also a natural necessity for the existence of a particular form of life. It is formed by consciously directed activity, but consciousness is only the auxiliary function of an otherwise deficient organic process. The human organism may be peculiar, but it is not utterly exceptional. In particular, it is no exception to the general rule that organisms are oriented to their own survival. If consciousness is, as Gehlen insists, an auxiliary means of the organic process, then its purposes are governed by the single imperative of assuring organic survival. Culture is the human form of nature in the quite specific sense that through cultural forms men fulfill their purely natural requirements. As much as for any more simplistic naturalism, the struggle for survival is the ultimate datum of Gehlen's anthropology. Within this scheme of things there is no valid criterion of right and wrong beyond the momentary requirements of the struggle. In its service, everything can be justified.

But Gehlen goes still further. Influenced by the *Umwelt* theory of von Uexküll, according to which there is a strict correspondence between the life requirements of a species and the way in which it experiences its surrounding world,[16] he argues that human consciousness illumines only as much as is needed for an improvement in the life chances of the species. To the extent that consciousness seeks to rise above the auxiliary function or believes itself capable of grasping a truth that transcends and so relativizes

16. See above, chapter 3.

the life struggle, it becomes, as Klages thought it always was, diseased. Readers of Plato will find this argument uncomfortably familiar. It recalls the positions of the Sophists against whom Socrates is compelled to avow that there are cares beyond mere survival and that in certain circumstances it would be preferable to die. More than anything else, Gehlen's endorsement of sophistic naturalism reveals the limitations of the politics implied in *Der Mensch*—limitations that will emerge more clearly when, in the next chapter, we consider Voegelin's renewal of the philosophers' appeal to the unseen measure of an absolute, world-transcendent, truth and good.[17]

For the moment, though, another line of criticism, that advanced by Ludwig Landgrebe, must concern us. Landgrebe is influenced by Heidegger's critique of the underlying assumptions of philosophical anthropology—a critique founded in the argument that human existence is fundamentally hermeneutic, in the sense that man's being depends not on any brute facts of life but on the interpretation he places upon the world. Heidegger talks not of "man" but of *Dasein*—literally, "being-there." *Dasein* is essentially the being whose mode of being is questionable to himself. Being-there-in-the-world is to live within a horizon fixed not by the sort of natural factors to which Gehlen appeals but, most basically, by the ways in which *Dasein* understands the open possibilities of an existence indisputably bounded only by his awareness of his own mortality. Human finitude, in this view, is characterized by what Heidegger calls man's being-toward-death, rather than in terms of the rela-

17. On this point, see in particular Eric Voegelin's discussion of the dispute between Socrates and Callicles in the *Gorgias.* Voegelin's comments reflect the experience of one who began his philosophical quest in interwar Vienna. His reflections on the moment in the dialogue when Socrates affirms that there are situations in which death is preferable to survival are of especial interest in view of the way in which the National Socialists utilized naturalistic, philosophical anthropology. "We feel the tension increasing towards the point where Callicles is co-responsible, through his conniving conduct, for the murder of Socrates and perhaps of Plato himself. The social conventions, which Callicles despises, are wearing thin; and the advocate of nature is brought to realize that he is a murderer face to face with his victim. The situation is fascinating for those among us who find ourselves in the Platonic position and who recognize in the men with whom we associate today the intellectual pimps for power who will connive in our murder tomorrow." Eric Voegelin, *Plato and Aristotle* (Baton Rouge, 1957), 37. Vol. III of Voegelin, *Order and History*, 5 vols. projected.

tionship subsisting between a certain type of essentially fixed being and the other more-or-less manipulable things of the world. Seen in this way, the exaltation of the life process and the struggle for biological survival to the point at which they become the absolute data, the ultimate reference point, for the understanding of human existence, is only one possible interpretation, and one that has quite specific historic roots in certain currents of nineteenth-century thinking. In Landgrebe's judgment, Gehlen's approach, by absolutizing a particular interpretation, not only precludes the possibility of political and ethical judgment independent of biological imperatives, but is prevented from comprehending its own historically conditioned origin: "the interpretation of the force of conscious self-knowledge and self-understanding as a mere auxiliary function of some organic process is itself no more than an *interpretation (Deutung)* which is posited by man in his striving to understand himself within a set of definite, already established historical conditions."[18]

From the standpoint of Max Scheler, it could be argued that Gehlen's anthropological conclusions only require the sort of supplement that could be provided if we widened his premises to include the dimension of spirit. Landgrebe's Heideggerian critique is more radical. What is required, he maintains, is not the addition of any missing dimensions of human experience but a reversal of the anthropological approach which, just because it is based on an anthropology that seeks a factual scientific grounding, necessarily starts from an inevitably partial, taken-for-granted interpretation of the nature of things:

instead of interpreting the self-understanding of man as a function of the facticity of life regarded as an ultimate, the interpretation of human existence—as a kind of life which by its very constitution excludes the capacity of answering the question concerning its meaning—must be understood as the function of a very specific manner of self-understanding. For a certain kind and amount of self-understanding pertains inseparably to human existence, and this understanding is more than a powerless reflex of a static constitutional condition of this existence. In his self-understanding man designs a

18. Landgrebe, *Major Problems in Contemporary European Philosophy,* 26.

blueprint, as it were, of what he can be and should be, and in doing so he reaches out beyond everything that he has been. It is precisely when the problems implicit in the anthropological approach are consistently followed to their conclusions—as is being done in exemplary fashion in Gehlen's treatise—that it becomes clearly evident why these problems are not and cannot be narrowly self-confined but point beyond themselves to a different plane, a plane upon which the approach to the phenomenon of man tries to derive its justification from the structure of human self-understanding."[19]

Considered as a variety of man's self-understanding, Gehlen's anthropology clearly shows its affiliations with nineteenth-century positivist attempts to interpret man as no more than a world-immanent part of an ultimately material order. Within their chosen horizon, such attempts are undeniably valuable, for in part man is just that. But the absolutization of the horizon, which finds expression in the belief that such an approach is the only one available to science, is not imposed by the nature of experience itself but only by the positivistic dogma that defines all knowledge after the model of the sciences of physical nature. This dogma is, in turn, rooted in a historical situation in which the physical sciences, and specifically Newtonian mechanics, seemed to have become the last refuge of certainty in a religiously and politically uncertain world. When, as Gehlen himself noted, the further development of the physical sciences became itself a factor contributing to man's uncertainty about his situation, the historically understandable restriction of science to the naturalistic model revealed itself to be an arbitrary and cognitively limiting superstition. Where experience, including the experience given in the artificial conditions of scientific experiment, is understood as a field of conflicting, more-or-less well-corroborated interpretations, appeal to the primacy of scientifically established evidence is displaced by an emphasis on the primacy of the interpretive process in which human existence consists. For it is only in the life process—the history of man as a self-interpreting being—that the available evidence of the nature of things and the things of nature is constituted as science. Science, including the sciences of man, is

19. *Ibid.*, 26–27.

part of a hermeneutic process in which man encounters not only the finite beings of the world but the mystery of Being as a whole. This means that, on the one hand, consciousness must be recognized as something more than an auxiliary function of an unquestionably given organic process; and, on the other hand, that the understanding of man and the order he inhabits must focus on the historical process of self-interpretation in whose imperfect light he builds his temporal refuge—all this without ignoring the significance of his organic form of life as a scientifically knowable being within a scientifically interpreted realm of nature. The *aporias* of Gehlen's anthropology can only be overcome by an interpretative philosophy of the constitution of order in history such as Eric Voegelin provides, while, in its turn, such a philosophy cannot afford to lose touch with the dimension of reality explored by the exponents of man's place in nature.

FIVE

THE DISCOVERY OF ORDER

In this chapter and the next, I shall be primarily concerned with the exposition and development of themes drawn from the political philosophy of Eric Voegelin. Voegelin's work, which amounts to nothing less than a renewal of the classical enterprise of *episteme politike,* allows us to answer the very questions on which Gehlen's anthropology is either silent or lapses into an appeal to the disorder and conflict of the struggle for biological survival: What is the right order of human existence? and, To what is man responding when he seeks to attune the order of his existence to a measure or standard perceived as inherent in the reality in which he participates? Voegelin answers these questions in a way that avoids dogmatism and relativism alike, and, at least in part, he is able to do so because at the beginnings of his inquiry—which coincide with the rise of National Socialism in the late 1920s and 1930s—he was deeply influenced by those very aspects of Scheler's thought that Gehlen rejects as remnants of an outdated and untenable metaphysics.

Gehlen, let us recall, accepts the broad outlines of Scheler's analysis of man's place in nature while rejecting the Schelerian argument that the essence of man's being is not to be found in the peculiarities of his organic existence but lies in his relationship as a spiritual being to the ultimate Divine Ground of Being. This argument runs through the second half of *Die Stellung des Menschen im Kosmos* and forms a crucial point of reference for the works in which Voegelin, writing in Vienna in the 1930s, sought to comprehend the disorder of his times. In the previous decade, Heidegger, as well as Scheler himself, had spoken of a crisis in man's knowledge of himself. The succeeding years witnessed a deepening of the crisis, and in 1933—the year in which Hitler became chancellor of Germany—Voegelin began his book *The Race Idea in Intellectual History (Die Rassenidee in der Geistesgeschichte von Ray bis Carus)* with the bald statement that "the knowledge of man has come to grief." The ideologists of race had resolved the crisis of self-interpretation in their own way, but it was a way that falsified the science of human nature to an unprecedented extent. Their appeal to the supposedly scientific baseline of a theoretical biology, whose inadequacies even on the level of genetic theory Voegelin well realized, denied the validity of the insight of classical and Christian philosophical anthropology—renewed in the work of Scheler—that man cannot be understood in terms of any single level of his being. The individual, Voegelin wrote, is a living entity and "not the puzzle-pieces of hereditary factors that he appears to be in genetics." Man is the epitome of Being, a unity of body, soul, and spirit. His nature is not comprehensible in terms of the natural sciences alone—not even a science which, unlike the theoretical biology favored under the Third Reich, is open to the fullness of the available evidence.[1]

Scheler's philosophical anthropology provided Voegelin with a critical standard against which he could measure the inadequacy of the biologically determinist anthropology expounded by the ideologists of National Socialism. The rejection of the naturalistic position that man is merely a peculiar type of animal engaged in the struggle for worldly survival—a view that is fundamental to the thesis of *Der Mensch*—formed the premise for Voegelin's critical reaction against the dominant ideas of his time. Although Scheler provided him with little in the way of a positive theory of political order, it was the final pages of *Die Stellung*—in which the question of man's relationship, not to the actuality of nature but to the Ground of Being as a whole, is explicitly raised—which seem to have set Voegelin on the meditative course that was to culminate

1. Eric Voegelin, *Die Rassenidee in der Geistesgeschichte von Ray bis Carus* (Berlin, 1933), 19, cited in Ellis Sandoz, *The Voegelinian Revolution: A Biographical Introduction* (Baton Rouge, 1981), 52.

in the great works of the postwar years—*The New Science of Politics, Anamnesis,* and *Order and History.* Out of the experiences of a murderous disorder justified by appeal to the supposed order of nature comes a body of work which, while moving beyond the terms of Scheler's anthropology and metaphysics, amply fulfills the Schelerian ambition of understanding man as more than simply a being of nature.

In the accomplishment of this ambition, Voegelin has produced what is probably the century's single most important contribution to the philosophical understanding of political order. If this fact is not yet generally recognized, it is because Voegelin's inquiry calls into question not only the premises of the ideology of racial determinism but every theory of the human condition, whether positivist, behaviorist, or historical-materialist, that confines its understanding of man within the parameters of naturalism. Since naturalism—broadly conceived as the view that identifies reality with the world-immanent materially based order available to investigation by the methods of the natural sciences—is the unexamined premise of twentieth-century political orthodoxy, it is not surprising that Voegelin's work should have been widely misunderstood. Too often it has been regarded as involving a rationally unjustifiable appeal to the teachings of a dogmatically formulated religion, despite Voegelin's trenchant criticism of the implications of the process of dogmatism, by which what are initially experiences of historically situated individuals become crystallized as doctrinally formalized, objective truths. One task of this chapter will be to rescue Voegelin from the charge of basing his theory beyond the bounds of either reason or experience. Only a philosophy like his, which recognizes reality as a process transcending the world as it happens to be, can do justice both to our experience of existing in a cosmos in whose recognizable form we sense a movement beyond itself, and to the life of reason that seeks to attune our conduct to a standard of right and truth by which even the factually existing orders of the world can be judged.

If, as I shall argue, the conflictual yet not arbitrary order of nature must in the last analysis be understood as only that lasting moment in the process of the real in which the being of man emerges, then only a philosophy like Voegelin's, which takes explicit account of the world-transcending dimension of reality, can open up the philosophical dimension that we need in order to appreciate properly the significance of the undoubted truths already disclosed by a naturalistic anthropology.

In recent years Voegelin's thought has become the object of increasing critical attention, most of it sympathetic and much of it of the highest quality. There exist today two excellent monographs, by Eugene Webb and Ellis Sandoz respectively, devoted to the systematic presentation of a life's work that is at once conceptually complex and concretely tied to the articulation of man's political experience as it reveals itself in history.[2] What I shall say by way of exposition of Voegelin's work cannot be a substitute either for a reading of these books or for the sustained attention that his own writings demand. At the same time, our inquiry into the nature of political order cannot proceed further without incorporating a considerable expository element. Voegelin's work is complex, and his writings are not yet enough known to render an element of outright exposition unnecessary in a book such as this. His works combine striking originality of presentation with philosophical and political concerns that are anything but new. Both topically and in the context of the history of our times, his work is closely related to the themes of the thinkers I have drawn upon in earlier chapters. But, in relation to their work, Voegelin's offers both a contrast and a complement. By allowing due attention to both the contrasting and the complementary aspects of matters, we may hope to deepen our own inquiry to a point from which we can see, as clearly as the limits of knower and known will allow, the outlines both of a perennial human condition and of a crisis of order that is original to our own time.

Before turning to the direct examination of Voegelin's argument, it is worth making a few remarks about the relationship between the theoretical exploration of order that we call political philoso-

2. Sandoz, *The Voegelinian Revolution;* Eugene Webb, *Eric Voegelin: Philosopher of History* (Seattle, 1981). Other works on Voegelin include Ellis Sandoz (ed.), *Eric Voegelin's Thought: A Critical Appraisal* (Durham, N.C., 1982); Stephen A. McKnight (ed.), *Eric Voegelin's Search for Order in History* (Baton Rouge, 1978). There is a full bibliography of Voegelin's work and of secondary sources up to 1981 in Peter J. Opitz and Gregor Sebba (eds.), *The Philosophy of Order: Essays on History, Consciousness, and Politics* (Stuttgart, 1981).

phy and the human political environment that is both its object and its existential context. Political philosophy is, wherever it is professed, a particular and quite peculiar event within the political order of human existence. While political existence is coeval with the life of the species, political philosophy arises under specific historical conditions. Specifically, political philosophy was born in the work of Plato and Aristotle, at a moment in history when the external, institutional order of the Greek city-state, the *polis*, had ceased to represent the embodiment of that order which the mind of the philosopher could discern as necessary to the accomplishment of the proper ends of human nature. The philosopher's exploration of the conditions of order represented a response to the established disorder of an unjust society, whose injustice was symbolized for Plato in the execution of Socrates by the Athenian state. Then and forever, political philosophy stands in critical relation to the human social reality in which it is professed—a point of great importance in understanding the original motivation of Voegelin's work.

We have already seen that human existence is characterized by features that make it ontologically distinct from other modes of being. This does not mean that it is set apart from the structures of the universe, but simply that it occupies a special position within the whole. The continuing existence of man depends upon the continuation of the supporting levels of inorganic and organic nature, which provide its material precondition; but the actual form of human society is created by the activities of a relatively autonomous element in the whole—man himself—in whose consciousness the subsistent process of reality is registered and experienced as a more-or-less but always partly intelligible order—an order requiring an active response from one who wishes to survive within it.

Man experiences the realm of activity as a field of real but finite freedom. Whereas this is obvious enough to common sense, the concept of a freedom that is utterly real and yet irredeemably limited tends to elude those more ambitious religious, metaphysical, and scientific world-views characteristic of civilized mankind. In my second and third chapters, I tried to show how such a freedom could be understood at the level of theory. This involved us in a discussion of ontological questions that are not often raised in re-lation to the understanding of politics. This discussion was neces-sary, for—since political order is only created and maintained through the continuous exercise of finite freedom—if we ignore the ontological questions that allow us to comprehend the place that such a freedom can occupy in reality, we risk misunderstand-ing the real distinctiveness of political order within the wider order of the real.

A fine balance is required if political order is not to be misunder-stood. We have to recognize that, while its achievement is the re-sult of the unceasing mental and physical activity necessary to hu-man survival, this activity is not only ontologically constrained but patterned in ways that are in large part culturally specific. Each of us comes to awareness of his identity and place within the world through the medium of a historically particular image of what is entailed by the real. To take a concrete example, the "I" who finds himself in a culture that is, by reason of past events for which he can bear no responsibility, dominated by the world-view of Islam is not the same as the biologically identical individual who might, had a certain battle gone a different way, have been born in his place. In this sense, the real world of political order may be de-scribed as an imagined but not an imaginary world. It is positively constituted not by the biological inheritance of race or species but in terms of the culturally enshrined symbols, the images, through which man represents what he conceives as the truth about the world and his nature as a part within it.

The simultaneous orientation of human consciousness to one-self and one's other, the world, is common to every symbolization of order. The representation of reality involved in this process is not arbitrary, for in every case the representation of self and world must articulate what man experiences reality to be. Thus every symbolization of order refers beyond itself to a level of experience preceding every expression—the level that Voegelin has called the "flowing presence," the stream of and through consciousness out of which sense must be made. The specific form in which a group articulates this experience is what we call its culture. When trans-mitted from generation to generation, it is called tradition. To be a cultural being is therefore to experience the humanly shared reality of the cosmos through the lenses of one's own tradition. Only when the view becomes opaque, when the conditions of life seem to deny the traditional representation of truth, is the inherited pretheoretical image of the world likely to be called into question. The starting point of a theory of order lies therefore in the experience of disorder and the unrest that this provokes in the mind of one who must endure it. Reaction to disorder can take place on as many levels as the malady itself, from the physical repression of seemingly arbitrary violence, through the construction of a counter-ideology of law and order, to the philosophical investigation of the conditions in which disorder can triumph. It is the last that is probably called political philosophy, and it appeared for the first time in the Athens of Socrates, Plato, and Aristotle. In the lives of these thinkers, the experience of inhabiting a disordered world was linked to the desire to understand and restore the conditions of ordered existence and, no less important, with a degree of conceptual and linguistic sophistication that allowed this understanding to be adequately expressed. In the hands of the philosophers, the Greek language proved a sufficiently supple instrument to permit the articulation in speech of the complex contours of social reality itself. Once in existence, the originally Greek science of order was potentially available to all, for while its reflections were provoked by the misfortunes of a historically specific form of political community—the *polis*—they rose from immediate concern with the particularity of events to a meditation on the universal conditions of proper order among men.

In this way, knowledge of the *polis* was refined into the science of politics. The pig iron of party polemic was challenged by the tempered steel of a new conceptual armory—an instrument of analysis and dissection derived from the language of political life and capable of being used for purposes of therapy as well as clinical demonstration. While the conclusions reached by Plato and Aristotle—on community of goods and on slavery, for instance—are open to reasoned challenge, the types of inquiry they practiced and the range of issues they considered relevant to political understanding set, once and for all, the standard by which every successor must be judged. Any conception of political science narrower than theirs must, by the fact of contraction alone, be judged as inferior.

The Athenian founders understood both the importance of the place of politics in human existence and the impossibility of understanding that place without reference to the physical and metaphysical conditions that structure man's life and make his activities possible. If man is, as the Greek philosophers rightly supposed, a being between god and beast, then politics as a field of inquiry must concern itself with a cognitive area extending from biology to theology. Now as then, the political theorist must therefore extend his considerations to issues that are usually seen as foreign to the narrower concerns of a positivistically conceived political science. In Voegelin's work, this breadth of vision is combined with the historian's attention to significant particulars and the philosopher's care for conceptual adequacy. It is this, rather than a taste for the empirically unfamiliar and the linguistically unusual, that accounts for much of the difficulty of his work.

Eric Voegelin was a theorist who devoted his life to the abatement of the mystery of political phenomena, not by the vain pretence that we can achieve a final perfect, institutional order but by steady inquiry into the relationship between the governing symbols of political life and the experiences out of which they arise. Starting from an intellectual ground shared with others—a clearing in the ideological jungle of the interwar years bounded by Edmund Husserl's phenomenological philosophy of consciousness, Scheler's philosophical anthropology, and Max Weber's rejection of every commitment in science but the commitment to intellectual honesty—Voegelin developed a theoretical understanding of man's political condition that is a decisive advance on those of his precursors. At the heart of this achievement is his clarification of the relationship of symbol to experience, for such potent political symbols as "Justice," "State," "Race," and "Class" are neither arbitrary labels whose "true" meaning could be settled by a philosopher's definition nor simple linguistic reflections of substantial realities that exist apart from the dynamics of human action. In politics, symbol and reality are inseparable. A nation, a race, or a class exists as an actor in history only in so far as the men who compose it conceive of themselves as members of the symbolically identified community. The symbols concerned are not the inventions of any philosopher but part of political life, moments in the process by which men discover sense or meaning in existence and order their lives accordingly.

Within the Marxist tradition, the well-known distinction between what is called a "class-in-itself" and a "class-for-itself" testifies to an awareness of this important point. A class-in-itself is a plurality of people who stand in a particular relationship to the means of production. When the members of such a class become aware of their shared situation—when they know themselves to be a "class" possessing a distinct class interest—they become a class-for-itself. Only then can the class play its appointed role in the drama of history. The class that does not identify itself as such—in other words, one that does not comprehend its existence by reference to the symbolism of Marxist class analysis—is, for practical political purposes, a dead duck. As we shall see, what holds for the Marxist theory of class is also true of ideas of racial identity. By purporting to identify the real basis of political community at a level of existence that precedes and underlies consciousness, the class or race "theorist" creates the symbols by means of which a politically effective community can be formed. The relationship between ideology, whether of class or race, and political philosophy is such that what the ideologist typically presents as the underlying structure governing events will be recognized by the philosopher as a mechanism for the mobilization of men for political action.[3]

Voegelin's friend and long-time correspondent Alfred Schutz attributed the difference between the social, or human, sciences and the science of the natural world to the fact that, whereas the realm of nature is without meaning to the entities that compose it, the social world is inherently meaningful to its inhabitants. In other words, an essential dimension of social reality consists in what men think it to be. It is on the basis of a pretheoretical, commonsense understanding of things—what Schutz calls the taken-for-granted reality of the world—that human beings plan and act. Out of this action, the specific form of the social world is generated. Schutz describes the patterns of meaning arising in the common course of life as "first level constructs." Such constructs form, in

3. This distinction plays an important part in Lenin's writings.

sum, a sphere of shared interpretations, a common culture that is as solid as it is unquestioned. Faced with the task of understanding such a reality, the social scientist has to develop what Schutz calls "constructs of the second degree." These are the interpretative frameworks that enable him to grasp and communicate the meaning-patterns that form, in every human society, the structure within which individual motivations and consequently actions appear.[4]

Voegelin's approach, whose classic expression is found in *The New Science of Politics,* is essentially the same. In view of its importance I quote it at length:

Man does not wait for science to have his life explained to him, and when the theorist approaches social reality he finds the field preempted by what may be called the self-interpretation of society. Human society is not merely a fact, or an event, in the external world to be studied by an observer like a natural phenomenon. Though it has externality as one of its important components, it is as a whole a little world, a cosmion, illuminated from within by the human beings who continuously create and bear it as the mode and condition of their self-realization. It is illuminated through an elaborate symbolism, in various degrees of compactness and differentiation—from rite, through myth, to theory—and this symbolism illuminates it with meaning so far as the symbols make the internal structure of such a cosmion, the relations between its members and groups of members, as well as its existence as a whole, transparent for the mystery of human existence. The self-illumination of society through symbols is an integral part of social reality and one may even say its essential part, for through such symbolization the members of a society experience it as more than an accident or a convenience, they experience it as of their human essence. And inversely, the symbols express the experience that man is fully man by virtue of his participation in a whole which transcends his particular existence. . . . Hence when political science begins, it does not begin with a *tabula rasa* on which it can inscribe its concepts; it will in-

4. Alfred Schutz, "Concept and Theory Formation in the Social Sciences," in Alfred Schutz, *Collected Papers,* ed. Maurice Natanson (3 vols.; The Hague, 1962–66), I, 48–66.

evitably start from a rich body of self-interpretation of a society and proceed by critical clarification of socially pre-existent symbols. When Aristotle wrote his *Ethics* and *Politics*, when he constructed his concepts of the polis, of the constitution, the citizen, the various forms of government, of justice, of happiness etc. he did not invent these terms and endow them with arbitrary meanings; he took rather the symbols which he found in his social environment, surveyed with care the variety of meanings which they had in common parlance, and ordered and clarified these meanings by the criteria of his theory.[5]

Political theory arises in the historical course of political existence. Theoretical reflection on the conditions of ordered life in society, exemplified here by Aristotle's paradigmatic enterprise, is provoked by perceived crises in the existentially established order of society. When things go well, the legitimating symbols of the status quo are usually effective enough in creating what Schutz calls the taken-for-granted reality of a meaningful existence. The mind of the social insider, the inhabitant of such a ready-constituted reality, is generally innocent of the fact that what he takes to be the "natural" way of doing things—by which he means the customary usage of his time and place—is no necessary condition of human existence as a whole but a specific historical and cultural development. Whereas every such reality is and must be founded in the ontologically given shared requirements of man's life on earth, each is a peculiar and unique achievement, for though the questions posed by the conditions of existence are anthropologically universal, the answers that men give are culturally specific. The world that man inhabits—the sphere of immediate experience that Husserl and Schutz, following Wilhelm Dilthey, call the lifeworld (*Lebenswelt*)—is culturally formed over history. Although ontologically speaking a human achievement, it precedes every individual whose birth it awaits.

The particular character of the life-world is, therefore, given to each future actor simply by virtue of the fact that he is born into it. Each has parents, grandparents, and so forth, back through the

5. Eric Voegelin, *The New Science of Politics: An Introduction* (Chicago, 1952), 27–28.

generations of the history of the species. To these he owes his physical existence and, almost invariably, his social identity. The actor lives from the beginning at the center of a web of social, economic, and political relationships that affect him in innumerable ways. Effortlessly he acquires a language, a native tongue, that allows him to converse with and learn from those about him. No less important, the language acquired in this quasi-natural way is experienced as a transparent medium opening upon the objective reality of the world. A native language, as it is experienced in the life-world, is a clear window upon surrounding reality. Words, familiar to a point beyond deliberation, "tell it like it is." With the mastery of language comes consciousness of one's social and even metaphysical identity, for it is through language that man learns not only who but what manner of being he is. Language is an encyclopedia and a catechism. Mastering language, the actor is himself mastered by the meaning-patterns that language conveys. Already placed spatially and temporally by the accident of birth, he learns through the unconsidered artifice of the native tongue what that place signifies and what chances it affords.

By means of language, man is made aware of a wider circle of contemporaries than he has ever met. Through chronicles and tales, he encounters his predecessors, whom he can never meet but who are nonetheless like him and whom he can picture and apparently understand. Contrary to what subjectivist philosophers from Descartes to Husserl have maintained, this is not primarily a question of understanding others by analogy with a primordially given self, for in large part a man's self-understanding reflects what he already understands of others. The self is not given at the moment of conception or at birth. It is a responsive achievement continuously formed in intercourse with the reality of the life-world. As such, it bears the mark of time and place, nature and society. The actor's very image of what it is to be a man derives as much from cultural as from self-experiential sources. In Hans Jonas' words, "Man models, experiences, and judges his own inner state and outward conduct after the image of what is man's. Willingly or not he lives the idea of man—in agreement or in conflict, in acceptance or in defiance, in compliance or in repudiation, with good or with bad conscience. The image of man never leaves him, however much he may wish at times to revert to the bliss of animality. To be created in the image of God means to have to live with the image of man."[6]

These general considerations help us to understand the circumstances in which Voegelin's early work developed during the years of interwar crisis. In one country after another, the framework of liberal constitutionalism and the rule of law shuddered or collapsed, in spite of the fact that, according to the wisdom of the schools, they represented the highest achievement of the institutional genius of Western man. Nowhere was the crisis so apparent as in Vienna, a city described by Gregor Sebba as "the enormous head of a tiny, mangled country which did not want to live and was not allowed to die. Impotent and hypersensitive Vienna reacted like a seismograph to every political or economic tremor abroad. This shabby, sardonically cheerful city was an invigorating cultural center of the first order, teeming with talent, ideas, experiments, hospitable to every kind of intellectual venture from the stiffly orthodox to the wayward."[7]

As time passed, it was the dark side of this freedom—a freedom to toy with and plan for every human possibility for good or ill—that became increasingly predominant. Re-reading Voegelin's writings of the time, Sebba describes them as evoking "the nightmarish atmosphere of those crucial years when it first dawned on us that the freedom of expression was becoming lethal to its practitioners."[8] Vienna, where in 1930 Sebba still found it possible to bring people of every different persuasion together for discussion, was the trial ground for ideologies whose logical consequence could only be murder.

Voegelin understood more clearly than most what was happening. From his earliest master, Max Weber, he had learned that "ideologies are not science and ideals are no substitute for ethics."[9] Karl Kraus, the great diagnostician of the corruption of language,

6. Hans Jonas, The Phenomenon of Life: Toward a Philosophical Biology (New York, 1966), 185–86.
7. Gregor Sebba, "Prelude and Variations on the Theme of Eric Voegelin," in Sandoz (ed.), Eric Voegelin's Thought, 3–66.
8. Ibid., 11.
9. Eric Voegelin, "Autobiographical Memoir," quoted in Sandoz, The Voegelinian Revolution, 38–39.

had alerted him to the consequences of the assault on the traditional image of man that he perceived about him. And in Max
Scheler's work he found a model philosophical anthropology—a
conception of the human condition which, while respectful of the
legitimate claims of natural science, envisaged the essence of man
as irreducible to any single level of his being. The creative appropriation of these influences immunized Voegelin against the temptations of the ideologies that suffused the atmosphere around him
and allowed him to see the inadequacy of every ideological formulation when measured against the critical standards of theoretical
science and compared with the philosophical study of man as it
had been practiced from Plato to Scheler.

The ideologies that pervaded interwar Vienna had deep cultural
roots and a readily comprehensible appeal. To the complexities of
a troubled existence, each offered its own all-embracing solution.
While capable of sophisticated expression, the ideologies of both
Left and Right were essentially simplistic. They purported to explain the complex configurations of historical experience and contemporary existence in "scientific" terms. Revolutionaries on the
Left appealed to a Marxist economic analysis of the contradictions
of capitalist society; those on the Right relied on the findings of a
selectively interpreted theoretical biology. The fact that the use to
which ideology put the discoveries of science was selective to the
point of distortion did not escape Voegelin's attention. In the immediate aftermath of World War I, his economic studies had already
led him to realize that, whatever its effectiveness in mobilizing
revolutionary consciousness, the Marxist theory of society and history was scientifically untenable. Now, in his works of the 1930s,
he concentrated his attention on the speciousness of the racial "science" of the National Socialists. Aided by conversations with emi-
nent geneticists during his visit to the United States, Voegelin was
able to show the inadequacy of racial ideology not only in comparison with the more philosophically differentiated anthropology
of Scheler but in relation to the very biological science in which it
claimed to find its scientific foundation.

Yet, as he also saw, it is one thing to undermine the ideologist's
pretension to convey a scientifically established truth and quite
another to make such an exposure politically effective. Ideologies

are politically immune to theoretical criticism, for it is not at the level of theory that they make their appeal. Furthermore, in an atmosphere in which untruth is pervasive the very effort to criticize ideological distortion is likely to be seen as just the preface to another ideological construction. In Jürgen Gebhardt's words, "Voegelin's early writings are permeated by the recognition that intellectual dishonesty is not accidental but is the very structure of reality of a social world he had to live in." This was, he later wrote, "an intellectual and social environment . . . no longer receptive to the rational, technically competent thought of the spiritually well-ordered personality." Awareness that such is the situation may provoke philosophical reflection, but it is necessarily frustrating to the philosopher's therapeutic purpose, for "if the realist should throw himself into the general mêlée as one of the contestants, he would defeat his philosophical purpose. In order to be heard he would have to surrender the standards of rationality. If on the other hand he has sufficient spiritual strength as well as philosophical consciousness to take his position beyond the disorder of the age . . . he will remain socially ineffective to the point of not even being misunderstood."[10]

It is a mark of Voegelin's realism that he never saw this plight as reason for compromising or abandoning the search for truth. Even in the short term, the breakdown of the intellectual and social conditions that make rational debate possible and effective need not make the situation utterly hopeless. There are levels other than the intellectual on which the forces of disorder and ideology can and must be fought, and these can be effective even when the defenders of order have no very deep understanding of the meaning of the struggle. During his visit to the United States, Voegelin was impressed by the extent to which the values associated with the biblical and classical conceptions of man had remained ingrained in the intellectual and institutional life of the nation. In England and America he saw societies, full of illusions no doubt, but peculiarly resistant to the appeal of extremist ideologies. The same type of constitutional arrangements that had proved so vulnerable to ideo-

10. Jürgen Gebhardt, "Towards the Process of Universal Mankind: The Formation of Voegelin's Philosophy of History," in Sandoz (ed.), *Eric Voegelin's Thought*, 70, 67.

logically inspired mass movements in Central Europe displayed, in America and England, a resilience that could not be attributed merely to their institutional form. When Voegelin later described the English and American democracies as representing "the oldest, most firmly consolidated stratum of civilizational tradition,"[11] he was pointing to the fact that, by reason of their relatively early historical development in the seventeenth and eighteenth centuries, the political institutions of the English-speaking world were not only well established in a temporal sense but bore the profound mark of the premodern concept of man as a more-than-natural being.

By contrast, he related the success of racial ideology in Germany to the fact that the historical formation of German unity took place at a time when a biologically oriented anthropology was in the ascendent. The creation of German unity had been a political process, but at the cultural level the image of what had been created inevitably bore the marks of its time. With·the defeat of the Wilhelmine empire in 1918, the political form under which a united Germany had been made collapsed, and the way was opened to an overtly racist political movement. There was, of course, nothing inevitable in this process—in politics and history, inevitability is invariably an illusion of hindsight. What Voegelin was pointing to was not a predestined trend toward the politics of race within German culture but the cultural fact that for readily understandable historical reasons the image of German nationhood was bound up with late-nineteenth-century notions of racial descent to an extent unmatched in the older established Western states.

Voegelin saw that race as a political idea—a symbol of self-interpretation and an instrument of mobilization—had to be distinguished from race as a scientific category. The social effectiveness of the first bore little relationship to the cognitive value of the second. However, in an age in which the appearance of talking in "hard scientific" terms guaranteed a hearing among an audience desperately searching for renewed certainty, the ideological claim that the two were identical was itself a powerful weapon. Study of the race idea sharpened Voegelin's sensitivity to the importance of

11. Voegelin, *The New Science of Politics*, 189.

the symbolic dimension of political life and led him to a new
awareness of the threat that dogmatic reliance on the exclusive validity of natural scientific knowledge poses to the philosophical
science of man.

In one of the first essays he published after his emigration to the
United States, he made his position plain. "The race idea," he
wrote,

> is not a body of knowledge organized in systematic form, but a po-
> litical idea in the technical sense of the word. A political idea does
> not attempt to describe social reality as it is, but it sets up symbols,
> be they single language units or more elaborate dogmas, which have
> the function of creating the image of a group as a unit. The life of a
> social group in general, and of a political group in particular, when
> understood in behavioristic terms, dissolves itself into individuals,
> their actions, and the purposes and motives of such actions. The
> group as a unit is not found on this level of observation. What welds
> the diffuse mass of individual life into a group unit are the symbolic
> beliefs entertained by the members of a group. Every group has its
> symbols which permit of concentrating into an emotional and voli-
> tional substance that which, if viewed empirically, is a stream of
> human action, articulated by behavior patterns and purposes, of
> highly questionable unity. A symbolic idea like the race idea is not
> a theory in the strict sense of the word. And it is beside the mark to
> criticize a symbol, or a set of dogmas because they are not empiri-
> cally verifiable. While such criticism is correct, it is without mean-
> ing, because it is not the function of an idea to describe social reality
> but to assist in its constitution. An idea is always "wrong" in the
> epistemological sense, but this relation to reality is its very principle
> and there is no point in proving it for every single instance.[12]

A political idea or symbol is not a means of knowing or understanding a pre-existing reality but of creating or maintaining one in
its own image. However, since ideological discourse purports to
tell men something about the world they inhabit, it must have
what Voegelin called "a material starting point" in some experienced feature of human existence. In the case of the race idea, this

12. Eric Voegelin, "The Growth of the Race Idea," *Review of Politics*, II (1940),
283–84.

source lies in man's biological identity as part of the animal world. Because man belongs biologically to the animal realm, "his procreative functions form a large reservoir of elemental data which may be transformed into unifying social symbols. The most obvious of the symbolic uses is the interpretation of a group as a biological unit by descent."[13]

The line of inquiry that Voegelin pursued resulted in a steady deepening of his understanding of the experiential base of political ideas and hence of the order which, as unifying symbols, these ideas constitute. Once it is recognized that political order is at all times constructed in the light of historically specific symbols of human self-interpretation and that these symbols have the function of relating the realm of action to the inescapable conditions of life, the content of the history of political ideas and the phenomenology of political existence—the twin foci of Voegelin's early work—are subsumed in something more philosophically fundamental—that is, a philosophy of consciousness that recognizes in "ideas" the symbolic indices of responses to experience. This philosophy of consciousness opens the way to a philosophy of history conceived not in the nineteenth-century fashion as a knowable story advancing toward a predetermined end, but as "an adventure of decision on the edge of freedom and necessity."[14]

This philosophy of history is articulated in the multi-volume work *Order and History*—a study of the symbols through which societies and individuals have expressed the common human experience of being active and restless participants in the wider universe.[15] Voegelin insists on the provisional character of all such cultural expressions. Inevitably, they involve the attempt to encapsulate the essentially unknowable in the medium of a language developed primarily to cope with mundane experience. Each man and civilization is conscious of occupying a limited place in space and time, and in order to make sense of this position, representative symbols must be developed. The function of these symbols is to establish intelligible links between the limited area of the lived

13. *Ibid.*, 284–85.
14. Eric Voegelin, *Israel and Revelation* (Baton Rouge, 1956), 1. Vol. I of Voegelin, *Order and History*, 5 vols. projected.
15. Eric Voegelin, *Order and History* (4 vols. to date; Baton Rouge, 1956–74).

present and the unknown transcendencies of the beginning and the beyond. Mythologies and religions, philosophical and scientific theories are all parts of this endeavor to understand the place of man within a whole that inevitably transcends experience. Voegelin came to express this constant feature of human existence through the Platonic symbol of *metaxy*—the unchanging structure of existence as the In-Between expressed in "the language of tension between life and death, immortality and mortality, perfection and imperfection . . . order and disorder, truth and untruth, sense and senselessness of existence."[16]

The effort to relate the limited area of experience to the inclusive order of being, which alone could give it meaning or justification, forces us to extend to that order the terms developed within the orbit of direct experience. At the same time, because we know that our pocket in time and space is not the whole of reality, the language in which experience is articulated already refers beyond itself, not only in an obvious sense to the extralinguistic reality of the world, but to a dimension that is transexperiential—the beginning and beyond of the process in which the world as it is experienced comes to be. Every extension of human experience expands the clearing we inhabit within the unknowable whole, but none can open up the view to infinity. For this reason, transcendent reality, in which the immanent reality disclosed in experience arises, is both unexperienceable and undeniable. As we shall see, the questions raised by this situation in which we find ourselves lead Voegelin toward a more adequately formulated endorsement of the Schelerian position that the distinctiveness of man lies not so much in his natural peculiarities as in his awareness of his relationship to the Divine Ground of Being.

When he wrote the first three volumes of *Order and History*, Voegelin believed that the history of symbolizations of order revealed a cognitive advance between the self-interpretation of what he called the "cosmological civilizations" of Egypt and Mesopotamia and the understanding of the human condition expressed in Christian teaching. In the light of his own experience and of his investigation of the sources and structures of the modern, natural-

16. Eric Voegelin, "Equivalences of Experience and Symbolization in History," in *Eternita è Storia: I valori permanenti nel divenire storico* (Florence, 1970), 220.

istic conception of man and the world, he came to realize that, in crucial particulars, recent centuries had seen a falling away from the clarity of vision that had once been attained. Such a view suggested a work constructed on the conventional linear, historical model, starting with a study of Israel and the ancient Near East, continuing with the Greeks, Romans, and medieval Christians, and on through Renaissance, Reformation, and Enlightenment to the crisis of modernity. "God of man, world and society," he wrote at the beginning of *Order and History* "form a primordial community of being," which is known to man "by virtue of his participation in the mystery of its being."[17] The characteristic symbols of the cosmological civilization already attest this community drawing its various elements into intelligible relationship by representing the earthly order of political society as a mortal reflection of the divine order of the cosmos. Awareness of relationship to, and dependence upon, a level of being more enduring than the moment of mortal existence is already fully present in the cosmological representation of order. To live rightly is to live according to the order inherent in the cosmos, an order in which earthly rulership—in Egypt the rule of the god-king, in Mesopotamia of the god's representative—plays its special part, for on the king rests the burden of maintaining the world's order in harmony with cosmic/divine order. According to Voegelin, the development of the symbolic languages of revelation and philosophy respectively permitted the deeper insight into this already perceived relationship between the human and the divine that found expression in Israel and Greece.

Israelite revelation and Greek philosophy bear witness to what Voegelin, following Henri Bergson, calls a "leap of being." It is important to be clear about what this term means. A leap in being appears, at first sight, to be a cognitive advance without ontological consequence. It does not transform the condition of human existence through a magical transfiguration of the nature and condition of the being who experiences it; rather, it constitutes an advance in insight that allows a deeper level of self-understanding to those who absorb its significance. In terms of Schelerian anthropology, it acts upon the psyche to bring about a change of spirit, showing the

17. Voegelin, *Israel and Revelation*, 1.

world in a new light and, as Voegelin argues, demanding of the spiritually renewed man a new, more differentiated symbolic vocabulary, adequate to the articulation of the new experience. Yet with Voegelin, as with Scheler, the cognitive and the metaphysical cannot be so clearly separated. It is not accidental that Voegelin speaks of a "leap in being" rather than an advance in consciousness, for though world and man remain ontologically unchanged by what occurs at the level of the psyche, what is in question is more than a naturalistically conceived cognitive advance. The leap in being constitutes a happening of truth in the world, a self-revelation of the Truth of Being that is experienced as the revelation of the world-transcendent God as the ultimate source and ground of all that is.

In *Die Stellung*, Scheler expressed this idea in terms of the opposition between life and spirit and the metaphysical structure of the process of being as it is realized through the interpenetration of spirit and life in man. "For us," he writes, "the basic relationship between man and the Ground of Being consists in the fact that this Ground comprehends and realizes itself directly in man, who, both as spirit and as life, is but a partial mode of the eternal spirit and drive." Recognizing his debt to Spinoza and Hegel, he continues:

> the original Being becomes conscious of itself in man in the same act by which man sees himself grounded in this being. We need but transform this thought, previously presented too intellectualistically, so that man's knowledge of being so grounded is the result of the active commitment of our own being to the ideal demand of *deitas* and the attempt to fulfill this demand. In and through this fulfillment, man cooperates in the creation of God, who emerges from the Ground of Being in a process whereby spirit and drive interpenetrate increasingly. The locus of this self-realization, or let us say, self-deification . . . for which Being in itself strives and for the sake of which it pays the price of the world as "history" . . . is man, the human self and the human heart. Here is the only place where the deification is accessible to us—but it is a genuine part of the transcendent process itself. For, although all things emerge in the process of continuous creation from the Ground of Being, from the functional unity of the cooperative interplay between spirit and drive,

these two attributes of the Being in itself that are known to us are related to each other solely in man as a living unity. Man is the focus where they intersect. The logos "according to" which the world comes into being becomes in man an act in which he can cooperate.[18]

Voegelin's notion of the leap in being incorporates much of what Scheler is getting at when he speaks of the realization of the Ground of Being in man. For Voegelin too, "eternal being realizes itself in time"; and it is in the time of human history that what Scheler calls the "ideal demand of *deitas*" is heard and articulated in the revealed word of God. Yet Voegelin's formulation is more metaphysically cautious than Scheler's, simpler and yet in some ways more elusive. Where Scheler attempts to provide, in the metaphysics of the interpenetration of spirit and drive in man, a metaphysical history of being as the becoming of God in the world, Voegelin, influenced more by Schelling than by Spinoza and Hegel, speaks only of the process of the whole as a mystery in process of unfolding, a process punctuated by revelatory happenings that have left their record in the words by which the philosophers and the prophets have sought to express what they have experienced and discovered.

It is the world-transcending nature of such experiences that compels the subject in whose life the revelation occurs to judge the original, cosmological symbolization of the community of being as inadequate, in the sense that it cannot encompass the felt presence of a Being experienced as utterly world-transcendent yet utterly present in the revelatory moment. Only the development of new modes of symbolization, of the symbols of revelation and of philosophy in its original Greek sense, makes possible the communication of what is, of its very nature, an individual experience. Only thus can the original event registered in the individual psyche— the experience of Moses at the burning bush, for instance—become formative for the life of a people. In this way, the potentially divisive experience of a psyche startled out of its old understanding can contribute to a people's sense of identity and place in the cosmos.

18. Max Scheler, *Man's Place in Nature*, trans. Hans Meyerhoff (Boston, 1961), 92–93.

Thus were the people of Israel formed as the wandering Hebrew tribes gradually came to reconceive the meaning of their existence in the light of trust in certain unique revelatory happenings. This, rather than genetic identity, lay at the origins of God's—and Hitler's—chosen people.

The cosmological civilizations found meaning through the symbolization of political order as analogous to the order of the cosmos. The order of society was understood to reflect the order of the heavens, so gods and men participate in parallel within a single inclusive scheme of things. Israel broke with this cosmological order by virtue of its experience of itself as a chosen people bearing a unique role in history. The significance of this break is that it acknowledges history as the dimension of change in time, and an essential characteristic of the cosmological symbolization is the attempt to deny the ultimate, ontological significance of such change. Typically, the renewal of the year and the cycle of the seasons are celebrated in archaic societies with rituals that are supposed to renew the order of society in analogous fashion. Such rituals testify, in Mircea Eliade's phrase, to a "terror of history"—a phrase suggesting at once man's unwillingness to admit the reality of irreversible change into the relatively comfortable cosmos of stasis or rhythmic renewal, and the threat of extinction that time and history embody. The existential basis of these rituals of world renewal is easy enough to understand, for terror is a feature not only of archaic man's stance toward history but of history itself.

"A civilization," Voegelin writes, "is the form in which a society participates, in its historically unique way, in the supracivilizational, universal drama of approximation to the right order of existence through increasingly differentiated attunement with the order of being." The consciousness of an individual or people is formed by the particular symbols through which this experience of participation is expressed. Thus "the men who lived the symbolism of Sheol, Desert, and Canaan, who understood their wanderings as the fulfilment of a divine plan, were formed by this experience into the Chosen People. Through the leap in being, that is, through the discovery of transcendent being as the source of order in man and society, Israel constituted itself the carrier of a new truth in history." This truth cannot be identified with the emergence of a his-

torical consciousness—the discovery of the one-directional, temporal dimension of existence. That had always been known, even
though its fatal truth had been mollified in the vision of a cosmos
governed by the rhythms of decay and renewal familiar from the
experience of nature. Rather, Voegelin insists, the new truth consists in the discovery of God as a source of order transcending society, nature, and cosmos alike. Once this has happened, no intracosmic reality, natural or cultural, can supply the ultimate measure
of truth.[19]

As Charles Maurras, the theorist and leader of the Action Fran-
çaise, used to argue, with this transcendental monotheism a new
leaven of disorder seems to enter the world—a permanent source
of political discontent based in appeal to a revealed truth beyond
and even opposed to the knowable imperatives of worldly survival.
The Hellenophile and culturally anti-Semitic Maurras saw an unbridgeable opposition between the world-immanent order represented by Greek polytheism and the world-transcendent discord
introduced into history by the prophetic appeal to the Divine Judge
of Hebraic monotheism. Voegelin firmly rejects any such di-
chotomy, even though he admits that with the discovery of the
transcendent God a new element of tension enters the picture. In
the first place, he argues, the break with the closed world of intracosmic harmonies is an advance in truth whose price must be paid,
for the leap in being involves a new openness toward an aspect of
experience that cannot honestly be denied—the experience of
man's inadequacy and of the inadequacy of every humanly created
political system when judged by the standard of the truth that man
discovers within his own soul yet knows to be more than his own
creation. Secondly, he insists that the sort of contradiction that
Maurras attempts to establish between Hellenic immanentism and
Hebraic transcendentalism fails to take account of the specifically
philosophical element in the Greek heritage with its own characteristic opening to a world-transcendent deity. It was not a Hebrew
prophet but Plato who wrote, in opposition to the Sophists, that
God and not man is the measure of all things. The later Christian
opposition of immanent reason to transcendent revelation, on

19. Voegelin, *Israel and Revelation*, 63, 123.

which Maurras depends, is not found among the Greeks. For the Greek philosophers, reason was a path, a meditative course, that led implacably to an encounter with the reality of a transcendent God, whose truth is not manifest in the factual order of the world but makes itself known in the philosophical symbolization of the Good, the Beautiful, and the True. In relation to the world, the voice of the Platonic philosopher, no less than that of the prophet, is a voice of witness and judgment. To fail to see that philosophy as well as revelation involves an opening to divine transcendence is, Voegelin insists, to deny the most precious contribution that Greece made to the theory and practice of order.[20]

Israel's conception of the realization of truth in history supplemented but never wholly displaced the older expression of participation through the cosmic analogy. So long as the Hebrew kingdoms survived, cosmological symbolization remained a vital element in the self-interpretation of the people of Israel and Judah. It was the historical drama of the fall of the monarchies, the end of statehood and the dispersal of the people, which further refined the Israelite experience and led, in the teachings of the great prophets, to the painful recognition that no concrete society will ever be the ultimate incarnation of divine order. In the prophetic books of the Bible is found for the first time the realization that "there are times, when the divinely willed order is humanly realized nowhere but in the faith of solitary sufferers."[21]

In Greece, the parallel experience of the breakdown of the order of the city-states led, in the persons of the philosophers, to an equivalent realization of the role of the solitary, spiritually aware individual—the philosopher or "lover of wisdom"—as witness to the true order of being. As we have mentioned, Voegelin points out that Greek philosophy knows nothing of the scholastic distinction between natural human reason and supernatural divine revelation. Reason, in the classic sense, is nothing other than the symbol by which man expresses his means of articulating the insight that the participating psyche obtains into the order of being; and there can be no intelligibility to this order unless it is understood as origi-

20. Eric Voegelin, "Reason: The Classic Experience," in Eric Voegelin, *Anamnesis*, trans. Gerhart Niemeyer (Notre Dame, Ind., 1978).
21. Voegelin, *Israel and Revelation*, 465.

nating in a world-transcendent source that can only be adequately represented in the symbolism of religious discourse.

It is not surprising that the philosopher's pursuit of elusive truth, although therapeutic in intention, is often seen as further contributing to cultural and political disorder. Philosophy challenges the truth claims of popularly accepted myths as well as the claim of society to realize the true order of human existence in its concrete institutional arrangements. As a symbolic expression of experienced order, philosophy is more supple than the compact form of myth. It allows a more differentiated expression of the experience of order and disorder but at the same time brings a new tension to the surface of human existence, for acceptance of the philosopher's pursuit of truth replaces neither the need for explanatory myths nor the mundane demands of social order. It is not that the philosopher is a natural subversive or agnostic, as Plato and Voegelin bear eloquent witness, but that his more differentiated symbolic vocabulary too easily identifies the cracks in knowledge papered over by explanatory myth and legitimating ideology. The philosopher is at best an uneasy conformist because, though he may recognize the social value of each, he sees the insufficiencies of both. If he is true to his vocation, he does this without arrogance, because the very way that leads him to his ultimate questions also teaches him that he too will never be able to tell the whole story.

In the first three volumes of *Order and History*, Voegelin showed that, while it was impossible to give any answer to the problem of the order *of* history, we could make sense of the past in terms of the discovery of order *in* history. No immanent directional logic exists in the succession of events, so the attempt to discover natural laws of historical development, in the manner of the nineteenth century, is therefore doomed to failure. History in that sense is without form or meaning. What is not meaningless is the continuing effort of men and civilizations to render their existence intelligible within the succession. History does not tell us that there is any necessary pattern in the unfolding of events to which the future, like the past, must perforce conform, but it does show that men have tried to discover such patterns, that their actions have been governed by the images they have conjured up, and that some of these have articulated the content of experience more ade-

quately than others. Past civilizations have meaning for us not because they were stages on the road to our own higher level of development, as nineteenth-century progressivism held, but because
each strove, as we do too, to understand the necessities and possibilities of existence in a world that is also our own. Such is the
common human quest expressed in the symbolic legacy of the past.

In volume 4, *The Ecumenic Age* (1974), Voegelin extended the
field of investigation to include symbolizations of order from beyond the Western orbit. The result was a considerable modification
of the original conception of the work, for the newly considered
historical configurations could not be arranged on any single time-
axis leading from compact to more differentiated patterns of symbols. Although he had always rejected any conventional notion of
historical progress, Voegelin's theme in the earlier volumes had
been the deepening in man's self-understanding between the cos-
mologies of the Mesopotamian empires and the Christian doctrines of man. The Israelite and the Greek leaps in being, symbolized respectively in revelation and a philosophy that was itself
revelatory of the transcendent, had broken the bounds of cosmological myth. The symbols of revelation and philosophy permitted
the articulation of distinctions in reality that had been blurred in a
world-view that conceived all reality, human and divine, social and
natural, as subject to the same cosmic patterns and rhythms. However, once the canvas was widened to include cultures beyond the
spiritual homelands of the West, even this limited time-axis became problematic. The single image of "history" seemed to dis-
solve into a multiplicity of histories, each structured by its own
characteristic movement toward truth. The prime task in the face
of this multiplication of histories became to explain parallel developments in cultures isolated from one another and to interpret recurrent patterns of symbolization in relation to the enduring form
of human life in the *metaxy*.

Modification of the original time-axis of *Order and History* does
not invalidate the insights of the earlier volumes. The fundamental
point that under certain conditions men may, but not necessarily
will, rise to a qualitatively higher understanding of their conditions
of existence remains intact. The tragedy is that only the experience
of worldly disappointment and defeat allows such leaps in being to

become effective factors in history. The revelatory occurrence in the psyche—the discovery of transcendentally ordered truth—can only become effective in reforming the self-interpretation of the social group when the claim of established institutional arrangements to represent divine truth begins to look distinctly tattered in the tragedy of their worldly fate. Because the success of a political order buttresses its claim to represent the one true order of human existence, it is political failure which, whatever else its costs, opens the way to the discovery that the truth of being lies beyond all institutional forms. This truth cannot be discovered in the forms of society or of nature but only in the depths of the soul to whom it is revealed. It is to the authority of such a truth that the Platonic Socrates appeals in his argument against the naturalism of the Sophists; and it is the same appeal that Voegelin makes in his struggle against the naturalistic ideologies of the modern world.

Christian teaching, Voegelin has consistently argued, represents a high-water mark in human self-interpretation, for Christianity presents a clear vision of the preconditions and consequences of that state of restless finitude—a finitude drawn to transcendence—that we experience as the normal state of our being. For several centuries now, however, the Christian symbolization of order and its concomitant anthropology have been challenged increasingly by ideological parasites that have grown up in their shadow.

Voegelin characterizes these ideologies, which feed from and falsify the Christian hope of salvation, as varieties of Gnosticism. In its original application, the term *gnostic* refers to a number of related doctrines and sects that flourished in the early centuries of the Christian era. They vary in their teaching and imagery but share certain basic features rooted in the belief that created nature is the work of an inferior or malign demiurge in rebellion against the one true God from whom spirit alone derives its being. The gnostic denial of the goodness of created nature implies contempt for the conditions that nature imposes on human existence, so earthly life comes to be regarded by the gnostic as a state of imprisonment of the spiritual essence that alone links man to his source, the one, true, absent, and alien God. Voegelin's interpretation of modernity in terms of a gnostic revival is not unprecedented. He refers to a work published in 1835 in which Ferdinand Christian Baur interpreted contemporary idealist speculation in terms of ancient Gnosticism. In the 1930s, Hans Jonas found a considerable affinity between gnostic teachings and the vision of existence contained in Heidegger's *Being and Time*.[22] Nevertheless, Voegelin's argument that such modern thought systems as Hegelianism, Positivism, and Marxism are fundamentally gnostic in their conceptions of reality is sufficiently startling and unlikely, given the characteristic worldly optimism of these systems, to present a major difficulty to those who approach his work for the first time.

"Philosophy," Voegelin writes, "springs from love of being: it is man's loving endeavor to perceive the order of being and attune himself to it."[23] The core philosophical experience, as philosophy was originally understood, is an experience of the tension between the disorder of the world and a transcendent order of being, registered in the soul, "the sensorium of transcendence," and articulated in equivalent symbols. It is this experience that justifies the philosopher's claim to tell man something about his nature and condition—something that the empirical sciences of nature, oriented as they are to the immanent state of things, are incapable of discerning. If the initial experience is denied, then the philosopher's words are only a game; and if the experience is not one of order, then the ordered and ordering properties of philosophical discourse are inappropriate to its expression.[24]

The gnostic, like the philosopher, is aware of a gap between the existentially established orders of society and nature and the requirements of a divine truth located beyond the world. But while the philosopher sees the relationship as one of tension in which, through man, the order of existence finds itself drawn toward attunement with the transcendent order of being, the gnostic perceives an unbridgeable chasm between the two. Gnosticism regards the created world as an opaque screen standing between the

22. Hans Jonas, *The Gnostic Religion: The Message of the Alien God and the Beginnings of Christianity* (2nd ed.; Boston, 1963), 320–50.
23. Eric Voegelin, *Science, Politics, and Gnosticism* (Chicago, 1968), 42.
24. This line of thought is the source of Heidegger's distrust of the philosophical tradition and forms the starting point for his "destruction of metaphysics." I have briefly discussed this in David J. Levy, "Heidegger, Poetry and Silence," *Poetry Nation Review*, VI (1979), 10–12.

spiritual essence imprisoned in the human body and the divine source from which it has become separated and to which it must return. This seems a long way from the teachings of the modern ideologies with which Voegelin associates it, but we must realize that the core of Gnosticism is a horror of being, a rejection of the conditions of earthly life as somehow alien to and unworthy of man. The *gnosis*—the knowledge that the gnostic seeks or believes himself to possess—is knowledge of the means of deliverance from these conditions. The literature of alienation, of which our age has seen such a profusion, is anchored in the same experience that led the ancient Gnostics to pray, in terms prefiguring the words of Heidegger, "Deliver us from the darkness of this world into which we are flung."[25]

Gnosticism arises in a genuine experience of the world, but one in which, as Voegelin puts it, divine mystery is misread as human absurdity. Reality, experienced as alien and defective, becomes the target of magical formulae or actions aimed at its denial or transformation. There is always a temptation to follow this path once the initial leap in being has occurred, for the break with the cosmological myth of immanent cosmic order takes the form of a revelation of the source of order as lying beyond the regularities of the cosmos. But this revelation—which opposes the transcendent God of the Bible to the intracosmic deities of city and field, and the originating God of Greek speculation to anthropomorphic figures depicted in popular myth—only develops in a gnostic direction when men come to believe that deeper insight into the nature of existence is capable of transforming the worldly conditions of human life.

Judaeo-Christian revelation and Greek philosophy give man new insights into his nature and condition by symbolizing his mysterious relationship to what surrounds and transcends him more adequately than the mythologies of Memphis or Babylon, but in no way do they alter the conditions of his being in the world. Leaps in being are cognitive, not ontological, revolutions. It is human understanding and not human nature that rises to new levels through them; consequently, they are reversible. Insights can be lost, and a

25. Voegelin discusses the relationship between Heidegger's thinking and Gnosticism in *Science, Politics, and Gnosticism*, 46–48.

lower, less differentiated level of self-interpretation may reassert itself. This is particularly so because it is always possible to misconstrue the leap in being as a step up the ontological hierarchy to the point where it is no longer necessary to take account of the trying limitations of the human condition.

Among the Hebrew prophets, Isaiah came closest to falling into this trap. When Judah was invaded by Israel and Syria in 734 B.C., and again in the face of Assyrian invasion some years later, the prophet advised the king to abandon faith in armies and alliances and trust only in the miraculous intervention of God. Consciousness of the transcendent God as a source of true order seems to have paralyzed Isaiah's instinct for effective action when faced with the all-too-worldly threat of national destruction. Of course, Jerusalem eventually fell to the Babylonians, but we may safely assume that the extra century or so of independent existence that Judah enjoyed owed at least as much to the royal dismissal of prophetic advice as to the plague that, on the second occasion, providentially or not, decimated the army of the Assyrian king.

Isaiah's derailment seems to prefigure later gnostic and ideological distortions of the nature of the leap in being. Voegelin emphasizes that

> the leap in being is not a leap out of existence; the autonomous order of this world remains what it is, even when the one world-transcendent God is revealed as the ultimate source of order in the world, as well as in man, society, and history. Isaiah, we may say, has tried the impossible: to make the leap in being a leap out of existence into a divinely transfigured world beyond the laws of mundane existence. . . .
>
> The constitution of being is what it is, and cannot be affected by human fancies. Hence, the metastatic denial of the order of mundane existence is neither a true proposition in philosophy, nor a program of action that could be executed. The will to transform reality into something which by essence it is not is the rebellion against the nature of things as ordained by God.[26]

It may be noted that only in a gnostic theology is such metaphysical rebellion justified, for there the conditions of existence are

26. Voegelin, *Israel and Revelation*, 452–53.

themselves conceived as the fruits of rebellion against the Divinity. Even so, the rebellion is doomed to fail. The mountains of the mind may melt away in the ardor of despair and hope, but the least natural hillock remains exactly what it was.

The intention of gnostic hope and despair is to deny this. Despair is rooted in the experience of being flung into an alien and hostile world; hope springs from the conviction that this world is somehow not truly real for one who has come to understand its alien character. The fallacy in this position is clear enough, for even if the conditions of existence were as necessarily oppressive as the gnostic maintains, there would still be no reason to suppose that they could be overcome. Voegelin notes that modern ideologists inherit the legacy of both despair and hope. The difference is that the modern gnostic tends to trust in revolutionary action as well as in liberating knowledge to achieve his purpose of overcoming reality. Yet liberating knowledge remains the basic element, even in modern gnosticism, since the assumption that effective world-transforming action is possible is based in a conception of history as a knowable process leading toward deliverance from the ontological condition of the species. Supposed knowledge of an inherent order of history leading man toward a higher level of being underpins the fantasy of metastatic action. Real history is a mystery in the process of unfolding, but in modern gnostic consciousness it is reconstructed as a succession of intelligible stages on the way to earthly fulfillment.

In the work of such nineteenth-century thinkers as Comte and Marx, exposition of the science of this imaginary history disguises the unreality of the metastatic scheme. Questions of philosophical insight, even more than divine revelation, are dismissed by these thinkers as "unscientific" and therefore irrelevant to inquiry. Since it is only such questions that can expose the futility of the gnostic's quest and the falsity of his conclusions, it is hardly surprising that he always receives from his inquiry precisely the answer he requires. The future state of mankind, teaches Comte, will be the Positivist haven of peace and industry watched over by the benevolent dictatorship of sociologists. Not at all, retorts Marx; it will be the kingdom of freedom, the communist cradle of a new humanity, rocked more or less gently to maturity by the dictatorship of the proletariat. I put the point crudely but not, I think, misleadingly.

In each case, the historical "destiny" revealed is a function of the component elements of the particular gnostic intellectual system. The elements of uncertainty and mystery inseparable from experience are excluded from modern gnostic philosophies of history as surely as they were from the elaborate mythologies by which the ancient purveyors of *gnosis* sought to explain the predicament of the spirit flung into this frightful world.

In using the term *gnostic* so widely, Voegelin intends more than to suggest an interesting analogy. Pretense to a certainty of knowledge not humanly available and radical dissatisfaction with the conditions of mundane existence are recurrent features of human consciousness; and the relationship between symbols and experience is such that the mental image of reality can be drawn in such a way as to exclude unsatisfactory features. Where exclusion is not possible, the importance of these features can be minimized by regarding them as historically transient and so capable of being overcome. For example, in the Marxist theory of history many of the definitive features of political existence are regarded as characteristic only of forms of class society that are doomed to perish. Time and again in Marxist writings, the blame for myriad ills is laid at the door of a particular system of ownership and production, as though human existence were structured by nothing more fundamental and constant than the peculiarities of a historically specific mode of production.

Although we may judge the gnostic's goal as impossible and his quest as vain, we cannot dismiss them as unimportant—if you cannot build paradise on earth, you can certainly construct prison camps for those who remind you of the fact. In this way, the recasting of the Christian hope of salvation in world-immanent terms is fraught with consequence, even though that consequence is the opposite of what is intended. You may not see that the nature of the material on which you work your purpose resists the form you try to inflict, but it is always possible to classify a particular individual, a race, or a class as the only thing now standing in your way, and to deal with the miscreant accordingly. Thus is the logic of murder spun on the wheel of self-deception.

It would be overstating the case to claim that this development, amply illustrated in the destructive achievement of successful salvationist regimes that promise fulfillment in kingdoms of freedom and thousand-year Reichs, is solely the result of a self-deluding movement of the mind called gnosticism. At the same time, the spiritual sources of disorder have tended to be underestimated in recent political thought. Self-interpretation, on which so much depends, is a more fundamental formative influence upon consciousness than self-interest, for only in so far as we have some conception of what we are can we conceive what we need or want. It is not the least of Voegelin's achievements that he raises the whole question of self-interpretation, considered as a universal feature of man's being and the source of its historical variety, to the center of political philosophical attention—which is where it properly belongs.

Six

REPRESENTATION AND TRUTH

The time has come to draw together the threads of what has gone before. This can only be done by defining as precisely as possible the tensions as well as the links between Eric Voegelin's studies of the historic route of human consciousness and the ontological and anthropological ideas discussed in the first part of the book. That there is a historical relationship between the two is certain. The figure of Max Scheler looms in the background of each line of inquiry—in the philosophical-anthropological investigation of man's place in nature as well as in Voegelin's study of the constitution of order in history. Both currents flow from a single Schelerian source, but neither from it alone. Even that source, the anthropology of *Die Stellung des Menschen im Kosmos*, has sometimes appeared, as it did to Arnold Gehlen, to encompass incompatible elements, a dualistic and inevitably speculative metaphysics alongside a scientifically attested study of the naturally founded human condition. So the question arises: Do we have before us two mutually contradictory visions of the state of man's being in the world, implying drastically different conceptions of the nature of political order, or are the two in some sense complementary?

As I have implied before, I believe that there is indeed a complementarity between the two perspectives. Moreover, this complementarity, marked though it is by undeniable tensions, is not the result of an accidental and partial convergence between philosophies based upon radically different premises—the naturalism most explicitly enunciated in Gehlen's *Der Mensch*, and the antinaturalism of Voegelin's work. Certainly the differences that emerge when we compare the two are radical enough, but the attempt to utilize both should not lead us into either irresolvable contradictions or an intellectually disreputable eclecticism. The tensions that exist between Gehlen's ultimate reliance on the primacy of the naturalistically conceived struggle for survival and Voegelin's appeal to the authority of a truth that cannot be encompassed within the world correspond to a tension that exists in experience itself—the tension between our fallible knowledge of the imperfect world of actuality (what presently exists) and our more certain knowledge that the actual (a moment in space and time) cannot be all there is to reality. An anthropology like Gehlen's and an ontology like that developed by Hartmann can well describe the structure of what actually exists in a spatio-temporal sense, but if we are to penetrate beyond that, as Voegelin's inquiry shows we should, we require something more. This need not be a formalized metaphysics such as Scheler envisaged, but it must be a philosophy open to the reality of what lies beyond the limits of actuality and prepared to consider the significance of any intimations we may obtain of the truth of the transcendentally real. Only within such a broader framework can the findings of a naturalistic anthropology and ontology be given their proper weight.

We know actuality as a state of affairs showing certain characteristics. We know also that each of these characteristics has a particular and, in principle, discoverable origin in the events of natural and human history. What is *is*, but once it was not. Everything we discover in the world came into existence under certain more-or-less knowable conditions. The stars, the earth, the living world, the species, each nation, and every individual emerged out of some preexisting state of affairs. The perceived finitude of everything that exists is, therefore, at its root a question of time more than of space. It is this element of temporality—a central theme in Voegelin's later writings—that leads us to recognize the limits of every ontology that seems to imagine reality as a structured system outside or beyond historical change. The truth of even the most generally valid ontology is implicated with the temporal contingency of its object; and since everything knowable is contingent, at least in the sense that it comes into existence in time, even the best-considered depiction of the structure of the real is, strictly speaking, true not of reality per se but of a state of actuality—an enduring moment in time—that may include, through historical knowledge, the once-existent actuality of a state of affairs that no longer holds. The contingency of everything finite is the negative side of what the medieval Scholastics meant when they said that God alone exists necessarily or, amounting to the same thing, that in God alone existence and essence coincide. Voegelin employs a more differentiated vocabulary than the Scholastics and, consequently, in line with common usage, prefers to reserve the term *existence* for the state of being of actual, finite items. He speaks, for instance, of God as the nonexistent ground of being, but this is not to reject the truth that the Scholastics mean to convey but only to replace a means of expression that can be bettered.

How, though, does such metaphysical stuff fit into an investigation of the nature of political order? This chapter will argue that not only does consideration of such issues improve our understanding of the conditions in which every political order is created and maintained, but it can also throw light on two major problems of political philosophy. The first problem is the relationship between the apparent constancy of human nature in a world made up of admittedly passing states of affairs. The second is the problem of representation. In the discussion that follows, I shall not only provide some sort of conclusion to earlier arguments, but I shall also give a framework within which to analyze the problem of political order as it presents itself in the circumstances peculiar to the modern world.

Before proceeding further, it is worth recalling that political order is a question of life and death before it is an issue for theory. Its theoretical investigation should be judged not only by its coherence but by its ability to throw some light on problems encountered in political life. If the questions raised in this chapter fall outside the scope of what is usually regarded as germane to politics, that is only because the broader vision of the human condition—an integral element in classical political theory—has been excluded from modern political discourse. It is on the work of men who reject such a limited vision that the restoration of political science depends. This too is a matter of practical as well as theoretical importance, for though a theory of political order is unlikely to make much direct contribution to sound practice in the short term, its long-term influence can be decisive. However abstract they may seem, theories in the human sciences have consequences because, regardless of the theorist's intentions, his work in clarifying and developing interpretations of human experience rises to the surface of affairs to the extent that it comes to shape people's perceptions of themselves and their condition. Unlike ideology, political philosophy is not so much an attempt to persuade as an invitation to consider matters afresh. Therefore its practical consequences, including any contribution it may make to the rational justification of any particular political program, are indirect, but they are not irrelevant to the prospects for society. Politicians who dismiss political theory as so much idle chatter are compelled to live and think, unawares, through the ideas of others. The sediment of past ideas is encrusted in the pipes of present practice.

A brief resumé of some of the philosophical-anthropological propositions advanced in previous chapters will make it clear why I choose to pursue my inquiry by examining the relationship between representation and truth. Because man is a biologically underdetermined being whose behavior is not fixed by rigid genetically inherited patterns, his response to the conditions of existence permits a variety unparalleled in other species. Furthermore, unlike other species, the conditions to which man is responding are molded to a significant extent by his own activities and those of his contemporaries and predecessors. The world of man is therefore inevitably a partially humanized world, the nature of which has been formed, though always within its implacably given ontological limits, by past activities. It is not that man creates either his own nature or the nature of the world, but simply that the effect of his actions always tends to emphasize and draw out certain naturally given possibilities at the expense of others. What these actions are depends in turn less on biologically inherited behavioral patterns, which as an aspect of nature fix only their possible limits, than on the interpretation that he places on his given condition. In other words, human action takes place within the natural/cultural universe, the life-world (Lebenswelt) into which each man is born. The already interpreted world into which each is born is normally

taken for granted as the unquestionable premise of life. Experienced simply as reality, it forms the baseline for all further questioning and exploration. But the reality of the life-world is not the
bare reality of things as it is known either to natural science or to
ontology. It is composed not by the entities and structures discovered through theoretical inquiry, but out of the common-sense images and symbols through which man represents what he conceives
to be the truth of existence to his own consciousness in the context
of his practical activities. This image of the real, which Scheler
describes as the "relative-natural world-view," always includes an
image of man as implicated in the world. Self-interpretation is,
therefore, an inevitable dimension of man's experience of the
world, even though, because it is normally the aspect of things
most taken for granted, it is the one least available to reflection.

Because human activity lacks the clear imperatives of instinctually given behavior patterns, the creation of political institutions
that guide, define, and limit activity is an essential part of man's
composition of the world. Institutions exist to guide human activity so that the sum of individual actions may serve the vital
need for individual and group survival in a potentially threatening
environment. But institutions can only do this if they in turn are
experienced as an intelligible part of the wider cosmic/historical
order in which they arise and on whose foundation they ultimately
rest. Institutions are culturally regulated and customarily regular
patterns of action, whose role in human life is to some degree functionally equivalent to that played by instinct among the lower animals. The symbols in which their existence is articulated must not
only name them but must tell those who bear and maintain them
something of why they exist. This does not mean that an institution need serve any specific purpose beyond itself, but only that it
must be seen to be an integral part in the economy of human life.
The existence of the family, for instance, is justified not on any
specific functional or historical grounds but in terms of the sort
of universal anthropological considerations that I examined in the
final part of the third chapter and which define in a limiting sense
the structure of human existence.

The question of truth in relation to political existence is raised
at the point at which I begin to ask not what I am to do but why.
Society urges certain lines of action upon me, but why should I,

who know myself to be endowed with the capacity for refusal, accept these urgings? If an answer to this question is to be persuasive
and socially binding, it must be couched in terms such as "That is
the way things are" or "This is the right thing to do in these circumstances." The *why?* that these answers will in turn provoke
requires a response couched in terms of what is taken as axiomatic
within the world-view of the particular culture. The ways in which
men justify their actions vary, but each, at least implicitly, embodies the claim that this is what a man—a "true" man, a "true"
Christian, or a "true" German—ought to do in a situation recognized accurately for what "in truth" it is.

Voegelin's work begins by recognizing that "the symbols in
which a society interprets the meaning of its existence are meant
to be true"—that society's claim to embody the truth of existence
is universal though variously conceived—but then it goes on to
show why such a claim is universally questionable.[1] Voegelin does
this not through a gnostic dismissal of earthly imperatives as evil
in themselves, but by analysis of the circumstances in which a
deeper level of questioning is provoked by the apparent limitations
of institutional order in embodying the very truth it claims to
represent.

Every humanly available truth must be imagined or represented
in order to become an element in the experience of the life-world,
but, Voegelin suggests, not every image is equally true. There are
not only unequal yet comparable levels at which man seeks to express the truth of his existence—essentially different ways of answering the recurrent questions inseparable from existence—but,
even at the same level, some formulations achieved in the course
of history express the truth about the human condition more adequately than others. However, it is in the nature of the case that
none is ever final, for the truth that the symbols of the society's
self-interpretation attempt to evoke is not the once-and-for-all
truth of a fixed and measurable state of being. Man's being in the
world has certain constant features, which are the brand-marks of
his specific variety of finitude, but as a whole the constancy of his
condition appears in the recurrence of existential questions of life
and death rather than in the endurance of what are always provi-

1. Eric Voegelin, *The New Science of Politics: An Introduction* (Chicago, 1952),
53.

sional answers. Every answer approximates as best it can to the ideal of a pattern capable of expressing the truth of existence, but it is the questions and not the answers that endure essentially unchanged in the unfolding drama of history.

To assess what has been Voegelin's particular contribution to our understanding of this condition, we must, as I have suggested above, relate his work to the positions maintained by other post-Schelerian thinkers. The choice of reference points is anything but arbitrary. Not only is Scheler's influence overt in Voegelin's early writings, but the subsequent development of some of the most important themes of Scheler's anthropology by men like Plessner and Gehlen explicates aspects of man's being that Voegelin himself tended to ignore. These are the aspects that concern particularly man's relationship to nature. Removed from the context of a mistaken naturalism, and hence no longer conceived as representing the whole truth of existence, the arguments of post-Schelerian philosophical anthropology articulate answers to an area of problems whose existence and partial solution is implicitly assumed in Voegelin's own work.

Nor is this the only reason for referring back to Scheler once again. In Voegelin's more recent writings—*The Ecumenic Age* (1974), in particular—we find a number of crucial passages whose meaning can only be fully grasped in the context of Scheler's work and influence. Our interest in these passages is more than expository. They not only represent the forward positions attained by Voegelin in his advance from the Schelerian baseline, which was his initial line of defense against the onslaught of racial ideology in the 1930s, but formulate better than anything else I know the limiting point at which the inquiry into man's nature and place in the cosmos is halted by the encounter with the ineradicable mystery of being. At this point, the problems of science and philosophy run up against the mysteries of religion. Stressing his continuity with the pre-Socratics as well as with Plato, Voegelin often described himself as a "mystic philosopher." This does not mean a professional concept-monger with a taste for the mysterious, but rather a seeker after truth—one who traces the patterns inherent in experienced reality to their limits, who finds that the lines of intelligibility lead beyond experience into the realm of the essentially unknowable, and who trusts in the analytical powers of the mind, expressed in the peculiarly self-aware symbols of philosophical discourse, to bring matters to that ultimate but necessarily incomplete clarity that consists in saying just what the mystery is and why it forms the horizon of knowledge that it does.

At the beginning of *Die Stellung des Menschen im Kosmos,* Scheler formulated the guiding questions of his life's work as "What is man?" and "What is man's place in the nature of things?" Provoked by the political success of ideologies that seemed to threaten not only the image of man but his very existence, Voegelin pursued a line of questioning that steadily and progressively drew out the metaphysical implications of Scheler's questions. Leaving to others the detailed study of man's place within the immanent orders of society and nature, Voegelin showed that the initial anthropological questions were ultimately unanswerable and even, in a sense, unintelligible unless placed, as the classical philosophers had placed them, within the broader metaphysical question of the origin and destiny of the universe as a process realizing itself in time—out of and toward infinity.

Let us take a passage from the final section of *The Ecumenic Age* to show how Voegelin's meaning can be rendered more transparent when placed in the general context of philosophical anthropology. It is important to note that not only are the origins of his theoretical work to be found in his utilization of Schelerian anthropology in the battle against ideological distortion, but that the conclusions he reaches represent an important advance on Scheler's own formulations.

In this passage the movement of the argument is, as it were, brought up short by a concluding statement so surprising to the consciousness of the modern reader that it seems to be not what it is—the necessary conclusion of a scrupulous argument—but an arbitrary dollop of mystical mumbo-jumbo.

"There is," Voegelin writes,

no "length of time" in which things happen; there is only the reality of things which has a time-dimension. The various strata of reality with their specific time-dimensions, furthermore, are not autonomous entities but form, through the relations of foundation and organization, the hierarchy of being which extends from the inorganic stratum, through the vegetative and animal realms, to the existence of man in his tension toward the divine ground of being. There is a process of the Whole of which the In-Between reality with its process of history is no more than a part, though the very important part in which the process of the Whole becomes luminous for the eschatological movement beyond its own structure. Within this process of the Whole, then, some things, as for instance the earth, outlast other things, as for instance the individual human beings who inhabit the earth; and what we call "time" without further qualifications is the mode of lastingness peculiar to the astrophysical universe which permits its dimension of time to be measured by its movements in space. But even this ultimate mode of lastingness to which as a measure we refer the lasting of all other things, is not a "time" in which things happen, but the time-dimension of a thing within the Whole that also comprises the divine reality whose mode of lastingness we express by such symbols as "eternity." Things do not happen in the astrophysical universe; the universe, together with all things founded in it, happens in God.[2]

How does such a conclusion find a place in the perspective of philosophical anthropology, with its twin emphases on the empirical science of life—physiology, biology, psychology—and on the equally empirical study of the workings of consciousness represented by phenomenology? In talking of God as the eternal reality in which the universe happens, have we not retreated from science into the language of a mysticism that is as repulsive to some as it is compelling to others? That will be the reaction of many, but there is another possibility. Perhaps the language that Voegelin found himself compelled to use, far from obscuring the reality of the objective situation of man, is necessarily entailed in the attempt to communicate the historical reality of what man's world-openness involves. It is, after all, worth reminding ourselves that it is only recently that the majority of thinkers have regarded it as possible and even necessary to speak of the structure of human

2. Eric Voegelin, *The Ecumenic Age* (Baton Rouge, 1974), 333–34. Vol. IV of Voegelin, *Order and History*, 5 vols. projected.

existence without reference to God or the gods. The superstitions of the present must not be allowed to define what we should dismiss as mere superstitions of the past. The historical record shows that the experience of transcendence is real enough, and the language and imagery of religion provides, if not the only way of evoking it, what is certainly its most vivid articulation.

In *Die Stellung*, Scheler sought to explain the significance of this experience. He argued that man's awareness of a transcendent Ground of Being—what Kant had described as the "condition of all possible experience and, therefore, also of all objects in experience"—is inseparable from his ability to objectify his environment as a knowable world. While the animal lives in the immediacy of "environmental spaces that vary with his movements . . . man," he wrote, "learns to reckon on a more and more comprehensive scale with his own accidental position in the universe, and with himself or his whole physical and psychical apparatus, as if it were an external object linked in strict causal relations with other things. In this way, he gradually constructs a picture of the world, the objects and laws of which are completely independent of his own psychophysical organism, of his senses, their thresholds, of his needs and their interests in things." Following Kant, Scheler maintains that in thus constituting the world in its objectivity, man discovers within himself an ordering center, spirit, which cannot be located in space or in time and which is, therefore, not a part of this world. "Spirit is the only being incapable of becoming an object. It is pure actuality. It has its being only in and through the execution of its acts. The center of spirit, the person, is not an object or a substantial kind of being, but a continuously self-executing, ordered structure of acts."[3]

While Kant and his successors had typically developed this insight in the direction of an epistemology that conceives the "phenomenal" world—the world as it appears to consciousness—as inevitably structured by categories primordially pertaining to consciousness, Scheler characteristically stresses what he sees as its metaphysical significance. He conceives the spirit that man discovers within himself and yet experiences as something apart from

3. Max Scheler, *Man's Place in Nature*, trans. Hans Meyerhoff (Boston, 1961), 46, 47.

his spatio-temporal place in nature as the realization in the world
of an aspect of the original Ground of Being out of which all things
come. Knowing itself to be apart from the world, spirit finds itself
to be directly related to the transcendent reality that founds the
very possibility of existence. To quote a passage that we have referred to before: ". . . the basic relationship between man and the
Ground of Being consists in the fact that this Ground comprehends
and realizes itself directly to man, who, both as spirit and as life, is
but a partial mode of the eternal spirit and drive. . . . The original
Being becomes conscious of itself in man in the same act by which
man see himself grounded in this being. . . . Man cooperates in the
creation of God, who emerges from the Ground of Being in a process whereby spirit and drive inter-penetrate increasingly."[4]

This position is, of course, closer to Hegel than to Kant. However, as Voegelin came to realize, once separate from Scheler's
metaphysical vision of the world-process in terms of the progressive interpenetration of spirit and drive, the Schelerian concept of
spirit in man—seen as directly oriented to a world-transcendent
reality of which it is, as it were, the worldly manifestation—brings
us close to the claims made by Platonic philosophy and Biblical
revelation, according to both of which divine truth makes itself
directly known to the soul of the human seeker, the philosopher or
the prophet.

In due course, we shall see the significance of this aspect of
Scheler's thought as Voegelin took it up. It was certainly not the
aspect that most influenced Scheler's immediate successors in the
field of philosophical anthropology. Two other elements in the arguments of *Die Stellung* provided the guidelines that his successors were to follow. The first was the insistence that man's nature
can only be understood when it is examined in the context of his
relationship to the world. This relationship is not contingent to the
essence of man but a necessary part of its composition. The Cartesian picture of man as a knowing subject facing the world purely
as a separate object of knowledge had to be abandoned because it
failed to do justice to the real ambiguity of human existence as a
being both a part of nature and apart from it. This, in turn, entailed

4. *Ibid.*, 92–93.

the replacement of epistemology, the theory of knowledge, by an ontologically aware anthropology as the founding discipline of any philosophical understanding of man. The second influential theme in Scheler's essay was, of course, the idea of ontological stratification itself—an idea that could serve as an explanation of the complexity of human nature as well as of the structure of the cosmos in which man participates as an effective but finite agent.

In 1928, the year that Scheler died, Helmuth Plessner published a book, *Die Stufen des Organischen und der Mensch* (The stages of the organic world and man), in which he rigorously examined the various aspects of the concrete relations that exist between particular forms of organism and their respective environments. In an earlier work, Plessner had already shown that, far from being passive receptacles of impressions, the human senses play an active part in the constitution of the world of experience. If, as Lockean empiricists and Aristotelian realists both argued, knowledge does indeed arise in sensation, this must be understood in terms of a sensory apparatus that is anything but passive. The sense organs are not screens on which the rude message of the world is projected prior to being processed and organized by the intellect; they are themselves "sensible media in the articulation of purpose, in the attempt to make sense out of the multitude of opaque stimuli."[5] Only in the light of this can we understand how, to use an example discussed earlier, the common tick is able to experience the world in a way that assures its survival.

Fred R. Dallmayr has summed up the argument of Plessner's *Stages* clearly and concisely:

each stage of organic life—from plants through animals to man—constituted a morphological structure or organizational form, marked by a distinct pattern of relationships between organism and environment. In the case of plants, this relationship is immediate and automatic, since there is as yet no differentiation between subject and object, between the agent of experience and the surrounding world. Animals, by contrast, are able to interact with their environment, by digesting impressions and adopting a variety of behavioural

5. Fred R. Dallmayr, "Plessner's Philosophical Anthropology: Implications for Role Theory and Politics," *Inquiry*, XVII (1974), 52–53.

responses. In Plessner's words, the life-world of animals is characterized by a "mediated immediacy" or "indirect directness." Their experience is mediated through their body with its sensory organs and
nervous systems; at the same time, their contact with the environment is immediate in the sense that animals coincide with or are
"centrally positioned" in their body and subject to the behavioural
chain of stimuli and responses. In the case of man, the relationship
is further complicated by his ability to be aware of and gain a distance from his situation. The human condition . . . is doubly mediated and "reflexive" by virtue of man's "ex-centric position" in regard
both to himself and his environment. Eccentricity, in this context,
does not mean removal from physical and environmental bonds; but
such bonds do not provide a stable ecology. Lodged at the boundaries
of nature, human existence cannot be reduced to a fixed content.
Facing his own alter ego man always points beyond himself, through
his capacity to question every conception of himself and his situation. Rather than being safely enmeshed in a life-cycle or the stimu-
lus-response nexus, man has to "lead" his life by designing a web of
cultural and symbolic meanings—patterns which provide him at
best with a fragile habitat.[6]

Plessner's emphasis on the need to exercise what is itself a free
activity, and on the essential instability of a result necessary to the
continuance of human life, is paralleled both by Hans Jonas' argument concerning the mutual dependence of freedom and necessity
in the economy of life, and by Gehlen's theory of institutions as
the necessary product as well as the essential condition of social
existence.

   In the present context, the significance of Plessner's argument,
as of the others, lies in his establishment of the existence of a specific relationship between the cultural sphere of symbol and meaning and certain distinctive features of man's physical and, as it
were, physiological involvement with nature. Such arguments
show that the historical and political world of human activity and
understanding is formally required, even though not determined in
its particular cultural content, by the position of man as a peculiar
species within nature. Of course, "nature" itself is a symbol, a term

6. *Ibid.*, 53.

of culture, and human experience is always the experience of one born to a particular cultural inheritance and formed within its universe of meaning. Yet it is not impossible to go beyond the cultural relativism that this would seem to imply, for underlying the multiformity of cultures is the relative uniformity of man's physical and mental equipment, the constancy of the elements composing the environment, and the consequent durability of the situation set up and maintained between them. In the durability of this situation lies the source of the recurrent questions that characterize human existence—questions that point to a constancy of condition in no way denied by the variety of culturally specific answers that are from time to time provided.

Admittedly, this durability is not a state of absolute uniformity or permanence. The range of possibilities available within the structured situation of being an example of *Homo sapiens* on the planet Earth, and not another sort of being somewhere else, encompasses every possible cultural and historical development, but not every one that is conceivable. So long as men are men and earth is earth, certain imaginable situations will be unattainable. The distinction between (logically) possible realities and (ontologically) real possibilities is inscribed in the structure of human being itself. We know, for example, that men will never be able to fly through the earth's atmosphere by the mere flapping of their arms, and, if our argument is correct, the impossibility of a nonpolitical existence is no less certain. To attain the one as much as the other would depend upon an ontological transformation of man and his position in the world, and that is something only the supernatural technology of magic would even pretend to attempt.

The durability of the relationship between nature and human nature is a function of the enduring of the beings involved, and this, of course, is not without a beginning or an end. So what is in question when we speak of the constancy of the human condition is not a matter of absolute changelessness but of a permanence of condition relative to the time-scale of human existence. The point I wish to bring out is that the level and time-scale of the cosmological and natural-historical processes—in which all particular types of being from galaxies to species are generated and which determine that sometime each will perish—are different from and more slow moving than the levels of group history and individual biography. Human history is not and cannot be a process of ontological transformation. Rather, it takes place within an already constituted ontological framework, and it is the enduring cosmological circumstance, generated at ontologically more fundamental levels of reality, that provides the real reference point for our well-warranted sense of the perceived constancy of the human condition. What is but a moment perceived from eternity may be treated as practically eternal by a species whose whole history is encompassed within it—a species which, furthermore, could not survive if the ontological preconditions which permitted its emergence were altered by a change at the cosmological level that is still its necessary foundation. So the character of historical events depends upon the natures of the beings involved, to whose constancy history itself provides subsequent and ample testament. Human history is not the creator but the consequence of human nature. Human nature comes into existence within a cosmological and natural historical process, but everything we normally mean when we refer to the history of mankind is consequent upon its emergence. Man is, in this sense, before history, which is, objectively speaking, only the field in which his possibilities are tried. Within the limits set by the present enduring state of the cosmological process, the particular character of human existence at any given moment depends upon the framework of self-interpretation embodied in individual cultures. Each of these is a unique response to a situation shared by all. Every civilization must be understood as a historical configuration—a product or effect— which comes into existence as a creative response to the situation that man does not produce but merely discovers himself as inhabiting.

Here we see emerging the solution to the twin problems of the relationship of change and changelessness in human affairs, and the possibility of there existing stable and even unchanging forms of being in a reality that is itself in process. What is commonly and, at a certain level of discourse, quite properly conceived as the interplay of change and changelessness in human history now shows itself to be a matter of varied yet invariable time-scales, which Voegelin calls specific time-dimensions or modes of lasting. Reality is the process in which being realizes itself in time; but this process is not characterized by temporal uniformity. Nature, as we said in our opening chapter, is a process in which natures, in the sense of specific essences such as the nature of man, emerge and crystallize until by chance or design they change or disappear. The process of reality takes this form because, although temporal to its core, the time-scale of its becoming varies between its ontologically distinct levels. As for absolute ontological permanence, that can only be predicated of the process of reality as a Whole or of the mode of being of one subsisting outside the moving drama of existence—one that Voegelin quite consistently designates as the *nonexistent* Ground of Being and calls God. The mark of His eternal, unchanging, and incorruptible being is His unreality as measured by the criteria necessary to intracosmic beings and processes, which, in order to be real, must be born into the process of things that He necessarily transcends.

Voegelin's analysis of the stratified, temporal structure of reality—in which the experienced constancy of one level is the measure of permanence for another, as a single human life might provide an image of changelessness for generations of butterflies—is one of his least noticed yet most important contributions to philosophy. The metaphysical issue of transcendence as an integral dimension of reality, which it opens up and wonderfully clarifies, does not, however, cover the whole picture, for within the process of the real all is not flux. Beings emerge—galaxies, planets, species, individuals—and these have defining characteristics that endure so long as the being itself continues in existence. We human beings inhabit the cosmos as one such species among others, and we require for our survival the continuance of just those conditions that initially made our emergence possible. Therefore no argument that leads us to a truer awareness of the metaphysical impermanence of the immanent order of things should be taken to deny the truth maintained by a philosophical anthropology that stresses the suprahistorical constancies of man's nature and condition. In the time-scale of human existence, within which all history is played out, the unchanging is as real as the mutable. It may be even more significant, for what does not change—the ontological structure of man's being in the world—provides the precondition as well as the limits for all real possibilities of life. The facts that define man's actual position in the world are at once so elementary and so universal that they form what is, in any relevant time-scale, a constant structure or ontological frame. I am thinking of such facts as man's erect posture and the consequences that this entails for his view of the world, literally and metaphorically, as well as for his ability to manipulate his environment by using limbs no longer required for locomotion.[7]

The direction of Voegelin's line of inquiry led him to leave explicit consideration of such matters out of his work. The result is that the positive content of his picture of the In-Between of human existence is less full than it might be. By stressing the experience of life as tensely strung between poles that seem to draw it beyond its own possibilities, he remedies the defects of a naturalistic anthropology, but, as he does so, he seems at times to devote insufficient attention to the cosmological boundaries of the human stage. Concerned as he has been to show up the fault in supposing the leap in being to constitute a leap beyond the necessities of existence, he has not, perhaps, marshalled all the arguments he might in showing why the world is so peculiarly resistant to the world-transforming ambitions of the ideologies whose influence he deplores.

On this point, at least, other writers seem to have more to say; and consideration of their work may do something to fill a gap in Voegelin's otherwise powerful argument. Philosophical anthropology and political philosophy require an adequate image of the immanent structure of reality as it is in the here-and-now of our native cosmos, as well as an awareness of the significance of the transcendent dimension. Knowing, as we do, that the political realm is always constituted in the light of symbols of human self-interpretation, we can, I suggest, understand it adequately only if we regard these symbols as responses to the experienced features of actuality—the factual here-and-now of society and nature—as much as indices of participation in a process transcending it. If this is so, then Hartmann's ontology of the actual, or something similar, may provide us with the essential complement to Voegelin's

7. See, for example, Erwin Straus, "The Upright Posture," *Psychiatric Quarterly*, XXVI (1952), 529–61.

philosophy of participatory consciousness. The first without the second fails to grasp the full implications of the temporality of existence and the transcendence of the real; but the second without the first leaves unexplored important elements in the structure of the world in which participation occurs.

Here we encounter again the second major idea that philosophical anthropology inherited from Scheler—the idea that neither nature nor human nature can be understood unless we conceive each as a composite of ontologically distinguishable yet existentially mutually implicated levels or strata of being. Scheler had distinguished the levels of inorganic or organic nature, psyche and spirit, but it was Nicolai Hartmann who developed this differentiation into a rigorous ontology of actual being. Forswearing all questions of ultimate origins and destiny, Hartmann pictured the world as a stratified whole composed of real and ideal beings in process, each determined in its nature according to its place in the whole and by the presence within itself of the various levels that constitute it.

When Hartmann writes that "the nature of man can be adequately understood only as the integrated whole of combining strata and, furthermore, as placed within the totality of the same order of strata which, outside of man, determines the structure of the real world," he is, I suggest, articulating the actual-ontological component that persists in Voegelin's more spiritualistically formulated image of man.[8] The picture of man as participant in an identifiably structured here-and-now loses none of its significance for philosophical anthropology when, in the light of further questioning, the here-and-now of the experienced order of things is shown to be only an enduring moment in the ontologically formative process of reality as a whole. Nor does awareness of the ultimate transience of every such state of affairs make its delineation any less relevant to the understanding of a human condition whose mode of lasting is that of individual and group life—a mode of lasting founded on, and temporally limited by, the endurance of the form of nature that makes human existence possible.

Scheler's image of man as an ontological unity composed of ontologically distinguishable strata—biophysical, psychical, and

8. Nicolai Hartmann, *New Ways of Ontology*, trans. Reinhard C. Kuhn (Chicago, 1952), 121–22.

spiritual—provided the young Voegelin with the structure of an anthropology to which he could appeal in his struggle against the terrible simplifications and distortions of the ideology of race. Although, as Jürgen Gebhardt has pointed out, the development of Voegelin's work led him away from the language and overt concerns of the Schelerian anthropology and ontology to which he then referred, our present reference to its own further development by Hartmann can help us to explicate some of the assumptions implicit in Voegelin's mature philosophy of history and consciousness.[9] This is corroborated by the fact that the vocabulary of stratification plays an increasingly prominent role as the argument of *The Ecumenic Age* moves toward its climax, where Voegelin seeks to express the reality of the Mystery of man's participation in the Whole as exactly as language permits. In the context of Voegelin's later work, the typical symbols of the theory of ontological stratification play a crucial role in bringing to light the temporal complexity of a process—the process of reality as a whole—that permits the emergence of relatively stable forms of being within its ceaseless movement.

Thus Voegelin formulates his understanding of the hierarchy of being,

> not as a number of strata one piled on top of the other, but as movement of reality from the apeirontic depth up to man, through as many levels of the hierarchy as can be discerned empirically, and as the countermovement of creative organization from the divine height down, with the Metaxy of man's consciousness as the site where the movement of the Whole becomes luminous for its eschatological direction. . . . The Mystery of the historical process is inseparable from the Mystery of a reality which brings forth the universe and the earth, plant and animal life on earth, and ultimately man and his consciousness.[10]

Close attention to the structure of the experience, as it is evoked by the symbols through which man has expressed his sense of par-

9. Jürgen Gebhardt, "Towards the Process of Universal Mankind: The Formation of Voegelin's Philosophy of History," in Ellis Sandoz (ed.) *Eric Voegelin's Thought: A Critical Appraisal* (Durham, N.C., 1982), 67–86.
10. Voegelin, *The Ecumenic Age*, 335.

ticipation in a reality greater than himself, reveals the paradoxical nature of the real as both a constant structure and an all-consuming process. For though the process of the Whole is sensed as moving in an eschatological direction—that is, toward its unknowable but certain end in oblivion or transfiguration—it is at every moment in its lasting structured in a specific and identifiable way. Human consciousness, which grasps the truth of its own passing and the world's, also knows itself to be founded in "the biophysical existence of man on earth in the universe." And, as Voegelin adds in a way that unmistakably recalls Hartmann's ontology, "by virtue of their founding character, the lower strata reach into the stratum of human consciousness, not as its cause but as its condition. Only because the strata of reality participate in one another, through the relations of foundation and organization, in the order of the cosmos, can and must the time-dimensions of the strata be related to one another, with the time-dimension of the universe furnishing the ultimately founding measure."[11]

Although the mode of expression has changed the image of man's place in the cosmos, what is conveyed here is essentially that which Voegelin attained some forty years ago and which he articulated in an essay, "On the Theory of Consciousness," sent to Alfred Schutz in New York. This is a crucial text that sums up the results of Voegelin's years of critical engagement with two contrasted but, as he thought, equally mistaken ways of thinking about man—the disembodied spiritualism of Husserlian phenomenology and the biopsychologism that characterized the work of the theorists of National Socialism. Then as later, Voegelin took care to describe the situation of man as a conscious actor within the world in a way that neither ignored the ontological situation of consciousness nor treated it as a determined effect of lower-level natural or biological causes. One passage in particular serves to illustrate the essential continuity in Voegelin's conception of the problem:

> Speaking ontologically, consciousness finds in the order of being of the world no level which it does not also experience as its own foundation. In the "basis-experience" of consciousness man presents himself as an epitome of the cosmos, as a microcosm. Now we do

11. *Ibid.*, 334.

not know in what this basis "really" consists; all our finite experience is experience of levels of being in their differentiation; the
nature of cosmos is inexperienceable, whether the nexus of basis be
the foundation of the vegetative on the inorganic, the animalic on
the vegetative, or of human consciousness on the animal body. There
is no doubt, however, that this basis exists. Even though the levels
of being are clearly distinguishable in their respective structures,
there must be something common which makes possible the con-
tinuum of all of them in human existence. The basis-experience is
further reinforced through the experience that this is not a matter of
a static complex but of intimate inter-relationships in a process. We
know the phenomenon of maturing and growing old with parallels
in processes of the body as well as the consciousness. And we
know—even though it is not transparent to us—the nexus of being
by virtue of which it is possible to "date" the succession of inner
illuminations of consciousness in symbols of external time. Finally
we are related to the transcendent world in the mysterious relation
of objective knowledge, a relation which phenomenology has by no
means illumined but rather only described from without.[12]

Alongside this experiential complex whose form can in large
part be explained in terms of the theory of ontological stratification, Voegelin came to emphasize the significance of the experience of meditation. Here consciousness, starting as it must from
the same ontologically conditioned state, reaches not toward
knowledge of the finite items and processes of the world but to a
grasp of the transcendent ground of being—that which *must* be in
order that any particular thing *can* be at all. To use the distinction
made famous in Heidegger's *Being and Time,* along this path consciousness is concerned not with beings—the immanent things
of the world—but with Being as such. The historical record shows
that the meditative experience, as much as the quest for ever-more
exact knowledge of the world, has its own characteristic content.
The search for the ground of being is not a steady if endless delving
into the depths of the psyche but a process punctuated by revelatory or theophanic happenings in which the transcendent ground

    12. Eric Voegelin, *Anamnesis,* trans. Gerhart Niemeyer (Notre Dame, Ind.,
1978), 28.

seems at times to project itself upon a particular consciousness, which experiences the event as an encounter with the voice of God. In making use of the Platonic conception of the soul as the sensorium of transcendence, Voegelin is employing an image that exactly renders the nature of certain historically attested experiences of men—experiences that happen in the world but are somehow not of it. So the outward journey of consciousness in search of the ultimate ground of its being finds an end where and when it experiences itself as the recipient of revelation. The terms that the human mind employs to express the ultimate source of all that is, are recognizably those in which the voice of God expresses itself in the records of revelation—infinity, boundlessness, eternity, power, love. The quest of the mystic, whose success no one can guarantee, leads implacably to the same ground where the voice is heard, even at times by those who, like Jonah, have no apparent wish to hear it.

Voegelin's ever-scrupulous use of the symbolism commonly reserved to theology seems, at first sight, to carry him a long way from his philosophical-anthropological starting point and from his explicit concern with political order. However, in drawing a picture of man in the face of ultimate transcendence, compelled to register dimensions of experience that he can neither evade nor fully comprehend, Voegelin is in fact doing no more than articulate more fully the implications of the concept of world-openness common to post-Schelerian philosophical anthropology. Man is open to the world, which stands before him as a field of potentiality, ontologically bounded, inviting exploration and compelling interpretation. He is neither the passive recipient of self-explanatory sense data nor the mental architect of the order he encounters in the world. Mind reaches out to what is not itself, but it must seek within, through the creation of appropriate symbols, for the means of expressing what it finds. If exploration of the structure of the world brings man up against seemingly unbreakable limits, interpretation leads him to the discovery that the existence of this structure, and his existence within it, are not self-explanatory but are grounded in a reality that lies beyond everyday experience.

The reality concerned—which is no thing of the world—seems at times to invade and possess consciousness as a manifestation of the sacred—the numinous or "wholly other."[13] Yet, in entering human experience, the "wholly other," without ceasing to be itself, enters into relations with consciousness. So the ground of being is experienced as a personal being or God. If we next ask how such an encounter is possible at all, the answer must be that consciousness is open not only to the immediate transcendence of the external world of objects and immanent processes, but to the ultimate transcendent Being, who is not merely the impersonal ground of immanent being but in some unfathomable sense a concerned partner in the affairs of the world. It is in this encounter that the philosophers as well as the prophets find the source of the truth that is subsequently counterposed to the established orders of nature and society as a measure and a judgment. An anthropology that denies the significance of this dimension of human experience is not merely arbitrary in its account of man but, more specifically, fails to provide a coherent account of the source of the judgmental truth to which political philosophy appeals.

How does all this relate to the question of representation? In *The New Science of Politics*, Voegelin speaks of man as a being who seeks to express the truth of his existence not only in propositions and myths but in the very institutional forms that govern his life. The argument, which underlies Voegelin's distinction between what he calls "elemental" and "existential" representation, draws on the double resonance of the term *representation* as it is used in aesthetics as well as in politics. Institutions must not only represent men in the legal/political sense of acting effectively for them, they must embody the essentials of the image in which the men of a particular culture recognize themselves and so, in a sense closer to the aesthetic, represent the beings whose activities compose them. The complex argument that underlies Voegelin's distinction arose from his observation that the mere existence of the forms of representative institutions of the West European and North American type was not enough to make them truly representative of the membership of other societies into which they had been introduced. Unless men see something of themselves or of what they

13. The terms "numinous" and "wholly other" are taken from Rudolf Otto, *The Idea of the Holy*, trans. John W. Harvey (Oxford, 1923).

desire to be in the political bodies that act for them and upon them, the institutional order cannot be other than a fragile shell. But what men are and what they desire to be is not an invariant factor. Once more we are back with the problem of self-interpretation and, specifically, with the fact that, for one reason or another, the self-interpretation that prevails in a society may be one that denies the transcendental dimension and with it the sole unchanging reference point for truth and order. Indeed, as we saw in the last chapter, Voegelin's interpretation of the ideological character of modernity emphasizes the extent to which the denial is built into the very form of the most influential schools of modern thought. The fact that awareness of transcendent reality and openness to divine truth are genuine human experiences attested by the historical record is no guarantee that they will not be dismissed as illusory. Where this happens, the prevailing image of man, and hence the model offered for emulation, can take one of two forms. Either man will be seen as merely another animal engaged, despite his ethical pretensions, exclusively in his own characteristic form of the struggle for biological survival, or he will be seen as a being uniquely possessed of a will to power to be exercised in the transformation of his social and natural environment and, through that, of his very nature. In both cases, the result will be destructive of those political conditions that make a fully human life possible. This, indeed, is what we perceive in the political culture of modernity, and it is to the specific examination of this culture that we must now turn.

SEVEN

IDEOLOGY AND
INSTITUTIONS

In previous chapters, the effort to examine the nature of political order in the light of philosophical anthropology led us to emphasize the constant features in the human condition. This is hardly surprising. The emphasis upon constancy, which, as we have seen, is not to be confused with absolute ontological change-lessness, is implicit in the anthropological perspective. Modern philosophical anthropology—like its classical precursor, the politi-cal philosophy of Aristotle—is an inquiry into the nature of man and into those features of his existence that, as the most general and the most distinctively human, may be considered as definitive of human being as such. The anthropological approach does not deny the fact of fundamental historical change. Rather, its focus upon anthropological constants serves to remind us that human history takes place in a natural and cosmological environment that has contours of its own. What I have called the space of politics is not a boundless vacuum, an unlimited arena for the projects of hu-man will and imagination. It is limited by the inherent structure of the natural reality that makes its emergence possible, and by the particular form that human nature has taken. The persistence of nature and of human nature is thus a presupposition of any realistic understanding of politics—that is, an approach to political phe-nomena that takes account of the knowable character of the world in which they take place.

At the same time, the nonidentity between anthropological con-stancy and ontological changelessness—which is evinced by the fact that the perennial truths about human nature and the human condition are precisely truths about a particular species that emerged and will no doubt disappear at a certain unforeseeable point in the history of the cosmos—means that the test of the value of the anthropological perspective is its ability or inability to throw light on specifically historical phenomena. An approach that stresses the constant features in the human condition can only prove itself by its capacity to aid our understanding of those unique and transient events and achievements in which history consists. In the context of the present book, this means that our inquiry must culminate in an attempt to illumine the peculiar and unprecedented state of political order in the modern world. In the second chapter, I remarked that "the existential state of technologically advanced modernity is . . . no more than the embodiment of a certain cluster of possibilities of nature and human nature." Now is the time to see how such a premise, which is at the same time a conclusion drawn from previous considerations, can provide a vantage point from which we can perceive the fateful limitations of a modern world that sometimes seems to imagine that it is free from fate and limits alike.

Let us once more set this analysis in its ontological and cosmological context. I have used the somewhat hackneyed metaphor of the stage—a bounded space within which self-regulating actors play uncertain parts in a drama whose future course they cannot know—in order to illustrate the point that, while there is an ineradicable element of freedom within the human condition, there is no freedom to step outside of it. The stage is set, and the action that has already passed upon it forms, at every instance, the unavoidable conditions for any possible future. This should not be taken to imply that the actors are mere puppets, unknowingly governed by conscious or unconscious forces outside themselves. Theirs is, so far as we can tell, a genuine autonomy. But the point from which the actor starts is never his to choose, and so each takes his place as an element in the self-sustaining tragedy of the real.

I call our drama a tragedy because, whatever the actors do, they can neither avoid the individual fate of death nor alter the fundamental structure of the stage on which the action is set. Here the metaphor of structure, with its unavoidably spatial reference, becomes a bit misleading, because the reason we may legitimately describe reality as tragic at a level more basic than that of the individual's life is that, as much as each life, the real is a process spinning itself out in time—a unidirectional process tending, through all the glories of its successive manifestations, toward oblivion. The fundamental structure of the stage of life is temporal, and any spatial constancies it possesses are constant only for a while and in relation to a being whose own moment of existence is more short-lived still.

It is worth pausing a moment to consider this, not in order to add another chapter to the chronicle of sentimental musings on the transience of worldly things, but because this tendency of even inanimate nature toward ultimate disintegration helps us to understand more adequately that disproportion between man's creative and his destructive powers, which has become obvious to an age that knows how to blow itself into oblivion and is fully conscious of the fact that, in the words of the conservationists' slogan, extinction is forever.

From Nicolai Hartmann's ontology, we have learned that reality is a stratified whole whose higher strata, in which life is found, depend unilaterally upon the existence of those below. The relationship between higher and lower strata is not symmetrical. The living being, for example, is absolutely dependent upon the endurance of a pre-existing physical world that his action is bound to affect and which he may, at the limit achieved by life in human form, destroy.

Destruction of the sustaining base by one who depends upon it *ipso facto* puts an end to his own possibility for existing; and the structure of the cosmos is such that a living being, possessed of sufficient ingenuity and insufficient wisdom, can undermine the very possibility of life. It is important that we understand what powers are required to bring this about. One does not end the possibility of life by killing living beings. That would not be sufficient. The definitive elimination of life on earth can only be brought about by the disintegration of the inanimate but mutable structure whose peculiar physical and chemical composition allowed life to emerge in the first place. While man has always had the power to kill what is alive, the power to disintegrate or transmute matter was until recently a magician's dream. Now it is a fact that must be taken into account wherever statesmen or scientists meet to project the future.

This is an absolutely new situation—a possibility of being that only the splitting of the atom has made actual. Its consequence is an extension of human responsibility to the point where the boundary between ethics and ontology has become obscure. The ontological imperatives still hold, which indeed is why the consequences of human action in the field are irreversible and definitive. Previously man has measured what he ought to do and be against the standard of an enduring cosmos or law of nature that escapes his control. But in raising himself to his present state of technological mastery, he has made himself responsible for the very survival of nature, including himself. So the relationship between the *is* of ontology and the *ought* of ethics has become hopelessly confused. The measure of the world is now submitted to the manipulation of man, and a formerly implacable nature is given over to the fallible wisdom of human stewardship.

For the first time, ethical judgment has become an all-encompassing matter of life and death. The limits necessary to our survival can now be transgressed, and beyond them looms the abyss of immediate oblivion. As Hans Jonas has pointed out, this existential *novum* not only forces us to a reformation and renewal of an ethics that, whatever its all-embracing rhetoric, was never designed to guide us in a plight that its authors could not have foreseen. It also makes us face up to the responsibilities of the stewardship that Jewish and Christian theologies have always conceived to be part of the human lot. "The boundary between 'city' and 'nature,'" Jonas writes,

> has been obliterated: the city of men, once an enclave in the nonhuman world, spreads over the whole of terrestrial nature and usurps its place. The difference between the artificial and the natural has vanished, the natural is swallowed up in the sphere of the artificial, and at the same time the total artifact, the works of man working on and through himself, generates a "nature" of its own, i.e. a necessity with which human freedom has to cope in an entirely new sense. Once it could be said *Fiat justitia, pereat mundus*, "Let justice be

done, and may the whole world perish"—where "world" . . . meant
the renewable enclave in the imperishable whole. Not even rhetori-
cally can the like be said anymore when the perishing of the whole
through the doings of man—be they just or unjust—has become a
real possibility. Issues never legislated on come into the purview of
the laws which the total city must give itself so that there will be a
world for the generations of man to come.[1]

It is hardly an exaggeration to say that the distinction between
social and natural reality is on the point of vanishing, not, as some
suppose, because science has revealed that society is subject to determination by laws of nature, but because nature itself has now
the existential status of an institution. Like the institutions of
political life, nature is necessary to human existence while being
largely dependent upon the care and respect that men accord it.
It is this situation that the ontology of stratification helps us to
understand. Eric Voegelin's reformulation of this ontology in temporal terms, which we examined in the last chapter, gives a more
dynamic cast to the ontological analysis of the opening chapters.
It allows us to express more adequately the inescapable truth that
the whole stratified system of the real is itself a vast and complex
one-way process whose movement is analogous to that of an individual life. By making this easier to see, modern science renders
untenable the archaic ontology of ultimate cyclical restoration. If
the cosmos seemed to premodern man a changeless or eternally
recurrent reality, that was only because the time-scale of its development from its physical origins to its end in what the physicists
call "heat death" cannot be measured in days or seasons. These do
indeed recur, and their recurrence is the obvious truth of experience. But they recur as features of an actually existing world that
is itself only an enduring moment within the overarching process
of the history of nature. It is the experience of the relative constancy of one stratum, such as inorganic nature, that traditionally
provided the measure of apparent permanence against which the
passing of living things could be set, so inorganic and organic
nature together could provide understanding with the image of

1. Hans Jonas, *The Imperative of Responsibility: In Search of An Ethics for the
Technological Age*, trans. Hans Jonas and David Herr (Chicago, 1984), 3.

a seemingly changeless stage on which human history was set. Archaic ontology, founded in the experience of a natural world whose very changes, known only in the regular cycles of stars and seasons, evince the changelessness of cyclical time, is the inevitable articulation of this experience. We, however, are the heirs of modern science and know that the cosmos is neither eternal nor self-regenerating. The appearance of permanence is no more than a millennial deception that we can no longer accept.

In a book published more than thirty years ago, the German physicist Carl Friedrich von Weizsäcker provided a vivid sketch of the universal unidirectional history of nature. Influenced by Martin Heidegger's view of the essential historicity of being as well as by developments in modern physics to which he had made a notable contribution, von Weizsäcker pointed out that the modern conception of man as a uniquely and exclusively historical being expresses no more than a half-truth. It is true that only man experiences history, for he alone is endowed with the consciousness that can grasp it, but he is at one with nature in undergoing history, conceived in the broad sense as the essence of what happens in time. Since nature develops in time, nature too has a history. Accepting the narrower view according to which there is only history where there is irrevocable change, von Weizsäcker argues further that, in this sense too, nature is historical. His words provide an appropriate complement to Voegelin's meditation on the root of our experience of cosmic constancy in our participation, not in a truly changeless universe, but in one whose changes occur at no single ontological level and on no one time-scale.

Von Weizsäcker gives the experience of cosmic constancy its due weight before cutting away the grounds of its claim to truth:

> In pride or in agony, mankind experiences the turmoil of its history—eternally unmoved, without history, the starred heavens look on. A stone that sleeps beneath the ground millions of years has no history—above it, historic life blooms and withers, hurries and grows. History is only where there is irrevocable change. The planets do indeed revolve in the skies, but for billions of years their paths have been ever the same. The planetary system is in constant motion, but fundamentally it does not change. Hence it is without his-

tory. The same seems to hold true of living nature. Every spring anew the woods cover themselves with leaves, and every fall they turn bare again. They are a symbol for us of the unchanging cycle of history-less nature. But man experiences events that separate past and present irrevocably. In himself alone, not in nature, does man undergo the basic experience of the historic: we do not step twice into the same river. But nature's appearance of being without history is an illusion. All depends on the time scale we use. To the mayfly whose life spans one day, man is without history; to man, the forest; to the forest, the stars; but to a being who has learned to contain within his mind the idea of eternity, even the stars are historic essences. A hundred years ago none of us was alive. Twenty thousand years ago the forest did not stand, and our country was covered with ice. A billion years ago the limestone I find in the ground today did not yet exist. Ten billion years ago, there was most likely neither sun nor earth nor any of the stars we know. There is a theorem of physics, the Second Law of thermodynamics, according to which events in nature are fundamentally irreversible and incapable of repetition.

This law von Weizsäcker calls "the law of the historic character of nature."[2]

In his fourth chapter, von Weizsäcker provides a lucid discussion of the Second Law and its implications for our understanding of the time-structure of the universe. Put at its simplest, the prevalence of the law in the conversion of energy within the universe means that every event in nature contributes, however minutely, to a running-down of cosmic activity to the point of "heat death," at which all motion ceases because all differences in temperature have been equalized. This is the state to which the universe itself is tending, notwithstanding the appearance of changelessness in the structure of nature. Heat death marks the point of cosmic stasis, the inorganic equivalent of the stillness of the grave.

From different perspectives, both Voegelin and von Weizsäcker bring us to an understanding of reality as essentially historical, and of history as a process that leads, in natural though not necessarily

2. Carl Friedrich von Weizsäcker, *The History of Nature*, trans. Fred D. Wieck (Chicago, 1949), 15.

supernatural terms, toward the stillness of death. Nothing that either says necessarily rules out the possibility of a divine salvation
or transfiguration—quite the reverse—but that would amount not
to a possible event within reality as it can be known but to an
utterly unforeseeable intervention by a necessarily acosmic being.
At this point, we may leave aside the eschatological possibilities,
for they can neither change our image of mundane reality nor
our conception of the place of politics within it. We must not, as
Voegelin puts it, "immanentize the eschaton" and, that being so,
we cannot but conceive nature as historical and subject to a fate
analogous to the death of the individual being. That in itself is
enough to explain the disproportion between the human's power to
create and his capacity to destroy, for in a sense an act of destruction is an act that furthers the most fundamental of universal processes, whereas to create is merely to form for a time something
that, once formed, is immediately subject to the disintegrating
pressure of the forces that determine the fate of the universe.

At the same time, the sense in which we are led to conceive
reality as historical makes us see why the experience of constancy,
expressed in the ideas of an unchanging human nature and a stable
natural order, is not illusory. That reality is ultimately a process
does not preclude its existence as a temporally bound system.
While everything that is real is impermanent in an absolute sense,
the relationship between the strata of reality does produce lasting
situations that allow viable species, societies, and individuals to
emerge. One such situation constitutes the human condition,
whose imperatives and natural parameters are no less anthropologically constant for being ontologically impermanent.

This condition is, so far as I can see, the specific fate of mankind.
To be human is to live within it and to be aware of doing so. It
is the same situation, which we have tried to express in terms of
philosophical anthropology, that was articulated before the development of philosophy in the language of cosmic dependence and
religious obligation. As we shall see, the fact that this situation was
once set within an archaic ontology of eternal recurrence is of less
significance than may at first appear. Whatever the ultimate destiny of the cosmos, the fate of one who must live within it in a
particular fashion is very much as archaic thought imagined it—at

least in the time-scale appropriate to the consideration of history and politics. My own reason for dwelling thus far on cosmological matters has been to explain the ontological significance of modern developments in nuclear physics and technology so as to bring more clearly into focus the specific objective novelty of modernity.

Modernity, according to Arnold Gehlen, is characterized subjectively by what he calls "the eclipse of fate." The phrase is both accurate and suggestive, for if there is one lesson we can draw from our consideration of the irreversible time-structure of the history of nature, it is that man's fate, while capable of being forgotten, cannot be avoided. At the same time, it is clear that a sense of unavoidable fate is not especially evident in the self-interpretation of modern man. This is what Gehlen means when he refers to the eclipse of fate in the modern world. Fate is eclipsed not because the implacable human condition has in fact been transcended—it has not—but because, for reasons primarily bound up with technological advances, men have largely ceased to conceive their existence as a matter of adaptation to the demands of the world. Instead, nature is, in Francis Bacon's vivid phrase, "put to rack," and the answers elicited are used to force nature into conformity with the demands of the human will. The question of the scientist finds practical application in the world-transforming scheme of the technologist, in whose success the beneficiaries of technological advance find evidence that fate itself has been transcended. Thus changes in the condition of life, often beneficial in themselves, encourage a way of looking at the world that is misleading and potentially catastrophic. Applied to politics, this manner of seeing things, which looks always for a means of transforming existence, encourages the growth of revolutionary ideologies while leading at the same time to a widespread impatience with the necessary disciplines of institutional life. The examination of these processes forms the main task of this chapter.

The idea that man is fated to exist in a certain condition, adapting himself to enduring circumstances that he cannot alter, has played a major part in forming human consciousness up to the present day. Its roots are undoubtedly found in the sense of dependence upon an uncertain and threatening environment that must have been the universal experience of our earliest human ancestors. The sense of dependence was, if anything, massively reinforced by the transition to settled agricultural life during the Neolithic era, when the awareness of contingency to an arbitrary and willful nature was supplemented and even in large part displaced by the consciousness that, through agricultural labor, man was participating in a world of regular and reassuring patterns. Chaos might always resume its sway—the threat could never be banished entirely, for the settled order of things was always vulnerable to human assault and natural catastrophe—but men knew that they could help protect themselves against such things by attending to the irrigation and drainage of the fields and to the state of the stockades and ditches that provided the homestead with a defensible environment. This was to play one's allotted role in the natural order of things.

Even now, the transition to agriculturally based existence has not happened everywhere. Hunting bands equipped with a stone-age technology—which, we should recall, embodies the effects of human ingenuity no less than our own achievements in electronics—share a moment in the earth's history with men for whom the typical structures of a life dominated by agriculture already belong to a seemingly irretrievable past. But this peculiar state of historical coexistence should not mislead us as to the significance of what is occurring in the world today. The balance between man and world has indeed been fundamentally altered. A mode of material existence that seemed until recently the inescapable lot of the mass of mankind is being eclipsed by the industrial and technological revolutions, and as this happens the structures of thought by which man has interpreted his existence and in whose perspective he has ordered his life throughout history are being undermined.

At the core of these threatened structures is man's sense of his limitations and his awareness of ultimate reliance upon something more than his own resourcefulness. The fact of finitude registered in this awareness has been a constant formative experience throughout the changes recorded in the history of human consciousness. The revolution in consciousness that Eric Voegelin calls "the leap in being" profoundly alters the sensed implications of this experience by relating man to a transcendent God beyond the mundanely apprehended rhythms of the cosmos. But the Deity who thereby reveals Himself proclaims Himself to be, even more than the cosmos that is now known as His creation, an ultimate reality on Whom everything depends. The change in consciousness involved in the leap in being is therefore something less than total. Like the intracosmic gods who governed the destiny of city and field, the world-transcendent God of the religions of faith summons man to conform to a pattern that is not his to change.

Gehlen is not, therefore, wrong when he claims that, in terms of the history of culture and consciousness, there are "only two decisive watersheds: the prehistoric transition from a hunting to a settled culture, and the modern transition to industrialism."[3] The first provided the existential precondition for man's discovery of the regular links of reciprocal service between himself and the creatures who share his world—a discovery that is central to his sense of active, intelligible, and nonmagical participation in a knowable natural order. The second, on whose implications we have already touched, eclipses this discovery of objective world-order by reducing the whole nonhuman world to the status of dependence on man. By undermining the self-evidence of an objective, suprahuman measure for action, the industrial and technological transformation of nature encourages the illusion that everything is possible. Ethics comes to be seen as a matter of subjective, ultimately arbitrary choice, and politics, the organization of communal life for the achievement of common purposes, ceases to be conceived as a field of necessary endeavor in the face of the pressures of the world. The new politics, embodied in the ambitions of revolutionary ideologies, is the politics of world-transformation—a precise equivalent to the modern technological project—which looks not to the conservation of nature and of human nature but to their ontological transmutation.

In aiming at the creation of a new man, the ideological politics of modernity draws upon that desire for removal to a state of unconditioned being that has, it would seem, always formed part of man's religious consciousness. Images of an original, lost state of innocence and the fall into the present state of existence are all but

3. Arnold Gehlen, *Man in the Age of Technology*, trans. Patricia Lipscomb (New York, 1980), 94.

universal, as is the expectation of an ultimate redemption from the frustrations of mundane life.[4] Such imaginings and hopes reflect a state of existential dissatisfaction that is, we may speculate, necessary to the survival of a species that needs to transform its environment if it is to flourish. Naked and instinctually deprived, primitive man must clothe himself and equip himself with artificial weapons and tools if he is to assure his existence in a frequently hostile world. From the perspective of his origins, the itch of existential unrest, though not constructive in itself, plays a part in impelling man toward the achievements of civilization. Today the same unrest and transformative impulse, having lost the countervailing pressure afforded by the evidence of a world beyond human control, has more equivocal implications. All too easily it can become the psychological source for a phenomenon—ideology—that is the political manifestation of what Heidegger has called "forgetfulness of being." On the axis of man's cultural development, creation and destruction belong together, for the same capacities and motivations that allow the attainment of civilization now push men toward enterprises that undermine all that has been achieved. Without the balance of an untamed world, only conscious wisdom can prevent this; and wisdom has always been in short supply.

The idea of fate, which registered the existence of inescapable conditions to which human life was subject, expressed the realization that all human action takes place in the context of a cosmos that not only makes such action necessary but whose autonomous processes consign all human achievements to certain decay and ultimate disappearance. Acceptance of fate, in this sense, should not be confused with fatalism. Whereas fatalism—the belief that the individual's actions make no difference to his worldly prospects—is a practically debilitating illusion, the acceptance of fate is nothing other than the realistic sense of one's own finitude. It is this sense of fate that allowed man to make the vital distinction between the world-transcendent object of religious hopes, the state of salvation and heavenly perfection, and the earthly, ontologically conditioned goals of political action. The eclipse of fate under-

4. On this point, see the writings of Mircea Eliade, and Paul Ricoeur, *The Symbolism of Evil*, trans. Emerson Buchanan (Boston, 1967).

mines this distinction and so allows the object of religious hope to be misconceived as a legitimate political goal and even as the immanent end of a knowable historical process. Where this happens, we have transgressed the boundary dividing the uncertain truth of faith—the substance of things hoped for and the proof of things unseen—from the certain illusion of *gnosis*.

In an age in which radical theologians like Jürgen Moltmann and spiritually intoxicated atheists like Ernst Bloch have taken advantage of our awareness that there is no constancy in the world that is not subject to process to assert that the *eschaton*, properly understood according to the lessons of Feuerbach and Marx, is a proper object of hope for *this* world, the opposed position must be plainly restated. It is based on the firm distinction between earthly fate and supernatural destiny. Religious hope is not concerned with the improvement of circumstances within the limits of a given ontological state but with an ontologically different condition—that is, in its most literal sense, with another world. If the imagined perfection of that world is misrepresented as a possibility of this one, its very desirability will cause it to be seen as the only worthy goal of political activity, for who will deny himself to the service of the highest good? Conditioned by the fantasies of revolutionary consciousness, whose fantastic character can only be revealed by careful ontological delineation of the meaning of finitude, political activity becomes a sustained exercise in the subversion of the only sort of order suitable to the mundane human condition—that is, the political order of institutionalized authority and authoritative institutions.

The unwarranted transposition of a religious theme into the key of politics is at the heart of the phenomenon of ideology in the sense in which I shall use the term. Ideology, so defined, is the original sin of the modern conception of politics. It designates a type of self-interpretation peculiarly related to a conception of political action as a means to the achievement of the essentially nonpolitical—because other-worldly—end of unconditioned being. Ideologically inspired action does not aim to change political order for the better but to abolish the conditions that make political institutions necessary. One who conceives political action in ideological terms sees its ultimate purpose as the deliverance of

man—or of a particular class or race of men—from the constraints
of political order. Ideology seeks the supersession of that order of
power that is, we have seen, an integral element of the human condition. Ideology is, therefore, revolutionary in the deepest possible
sense. Its very adoption, made possible by the eclipse of fate—itself
the consequence of a misunderstanding of the significance of human agency—is an act of rebellion against conditions that are, if
there has been any truth in our argument, necessary features of
human existence. In whatsoever name it speaks, ideology is perni-
cious because it undermines our sense of the necessity of politics
by holding out the false promise of a postpolitical world.

The consequences of thus confusing the uncertainties of a supernatural destiny, for whose reality we can have only the evidence of
faith, with the certainty of man's natural fate are clear. If man's is
essentially a political condition, and if the common project of ideology is the abolition of politics, albeit by political means, then the
ideological project must ever be frustrated. But while an ideology's
positive goal can never be achieved, its prevalence in the mind of a
man or of an age can be sufficient to disrupt and destroy the cultural and institutional conditions necessary to the conservation of
what Aristotle called the good life. To illustrate this, we have only
to consider the measures of general surveillance and violent repression that may be forced upon the government of a nation that finds
itself disrupted by the activities of ideologically motivated terror-
ists. Three undeniable propositions define the problem. First, the
suppression of terrorism is a responsibility that no government can
avoid. Second, the existence of revolutionary ideologies provides a
permanent source of motivation for this terrorism. Finally, the defeat of such terrorism cannot be accomplished without cost to the
good life. This is a measure of the destruction that even the failures
of ideology can wreak.

Where ideologically motivated action actually succeeds in bringing to power a regime dedicated to the achievement of the goal of
postpolitical existence—for example, the abolition of rulership or
the spontaneous community of a socially undifferentiated race or
class—the result will be the construction of a totalitarian system
of social control. This must be attempted even where it is not
desired, for the ideological state—unable to realize its goals yet

incapable of abandoning them without disowning its sole *raison d'être*, at war with reality itself—must encompass itself with a fabric of manipulation and pretense that can buttress its legitimacy by making it appear that the impossible is in the course of being achieved. Silence is the least of the penalties inflicted on those who remain unconvinced. The very success of an ideology is hollow, leading not to the attainment of its intended goals but to the dominion of lies and the suppression of every project that might discover the fraud that the original fantasy must inevitably become.

This phenomenon is best exemplified in the record of the Soviet Union, where the gap between libertarian intention and repressive achievement is greatest. The USSR, committed by its origins and founding ideology to the attainment of the postpolitical state of "communism" through the socialization of the means of production, is caught in what one can only call an ideological trap. The essential feature of a good trap is that it is all but inescapable. Once caught, the victim's efforts to escape are fruitless because an efficient trap is so constructed that the struggle to break loose only enmeshes the victim further. The ideological trap is not dissimilar. The more measures the regime takes in order to realize its projected goals—for instance, the socialization of production and the institution of an all-embracing system of centralized economic planning as the socialist precondition for the attainment of communist freedom—the less it can turn back on its path. And this effort must continue in spite of the fact that socialism of the Marxist-Leninist type can be seen to further neither political freedom nor economic plenty. In an ideological state, no one can learn from such failures, for however unfortunate the consequences of ideologically motivated policies, an essentially ideological state—one whose sole legitimacy rests on its promise to fulfill unachievable goals—cannot admit that the policies that are supposed to realize its central goals are mistaken.

Those who seek to draw a line between the historical experience of Soviet socialism as it has emerged since 1917 and the original Marxian idea that socialization of the economy would provide the framework and foundation for a qualitatively higher form of life are mistaken. They forget that, regardless of whether or not the leaders of the USSR read Marx's writings with the same devotion as his

Western commentators, the projects they have pursued at home and abroad are uniquely consistent with his analysis. Marxists may differ about the method and timing of socialization, but it is hard to see how any of them could admit that the idea itself was essentially misconceived, that it was never more than a self-defeating means to the unreal end of postpolitical communism. To disown the socialist path would be to dispense with the central strut in the Marxist economy of salvation, for what is it that distinguishes Marx's writings from those he regarded as merely "utopian" if not his claim to have discovered that the key to human fulfillment lies in the elimination of private property in the means of production? This, both he and Engels maintained, was the sure and only way to attain the cherished autonomy imagined but vainly sought by idealist philosophers. If Marx's "discovery" turns out to be fool's gold, all that remains of his work is some perceptive political journalism, the dubious social psychology of "alienation," and a tendentious analysis of the workings of the mid-nineteenth-century economy.[5]

It would be unfortunate if we fixed our attention too exclusively on Marxism, which is no more than the pre-eminent example of the practical utopianism that corrupts the political imagination of the modern world. We cannot understand the relationship between ideology and the present crisis of institutions without sketching in something of the cultural history of modernity, and even a brief sketch will reveal that the dimensions of our problem are wider than concern with an overtly revolutionary ideology could suggest. We must try to identify the flaws in an anthropology that Marxists share with many of their professed opponents. Diagnosis of the preconditions and consequences of the eclipse of fate will provide us with further support for our vindication of the claims of political order to be the proper and permanent order of human existence.

What I wish to argue is that, to understand the present predicament of political order, we have to understand modernity as being primarily a state of existence, a novel civilization peculiarly forgetful of ontological exigencies that it only apparently transcends. This forgetfulness is neither a chance development nor is it im-

5. The best single survey of the Marxist tradition as a whole is Leszek Kolakowski, *Main Currents of Marxism: Its, Rise, Growth, and Dissolution* (3 vols.; Oxford, 1980).

placably determined. Rather, we must understand it as a likely but not a necessary response to a situation in which human life is more than ever removed from the evidence of its contingency to something greater than itself. In the absence of such evidence, the constitutive limitations of finite human being come to be experienced as frustrating curbs upon the projects of the will. Existential unrest then becomes politically effective in the form of ideological politics, with all the consequences that I have suggested.

The argument that technological advance tends to encourage specific illusions in human self-interpretation is not uncommon today. However, such orthodoxy as there is in such matters is still, I believe, close to the view of nineteenth-century progressivism, according to which there was an intimate and positive connection between man's capacity to control his immediate environment and his level of self-understanding. The progressivists believed that the "savage," with his primitive technology, lived in a world of illusions, peopled with imaginary spirits and governed by uncomprehended forces; the scientifically informed sophisticate, in contrast, understood his environment to the extent that he had learned to control it, recognizing himself to be both an integral part of that environment and its potential master. The criticism of this view, according to which technological advance and human understanding progress hand in hand, is not to be confused with the homespun romanticism that finds fault with the advance of technology as such. That, as much as the utopian quest for unconditioned being, is a denial of the historical fate of man as a creature whose life depends upon mastery of his surroundings. The target of our criticism is not technology itself but certain habits of thought that tend to thrive in an environment insulated by technological advance from the evidence of dependence and finitude. The purpose of criticism is, by the same token, not to recommend the resurrection of a life-style that is past but to improve in some small way the prospects of one that is presently endangered by the misunderstanding of its predicament.

The truth about the human condition is not progressively disclosed as a cognitive by-product of man's technologically triumphant march through time. It is realized always incompletely and only in the form of insights and intimations of fundamental dependence. In view of this, we should not be surprised if the very limitations of past technology played their part in promoting a truer conception of the human condition than that which typically prevails today. It was in the light of such a view of things that human beings come to create and cherish institutions whose anthropological value far outlasts the conditions of their creation.

Arnold Gehlen has pointed out that a form of existence in which human life was clearly dependent upon the cultivation of the soil encouraged the development of structures of thought and the formation of institutions that remain indispensible to the preservation of civilization under all circumstances. Property, law, and the impartially authoritative state can all be traced to such roots. Men learn the significance of the interdependence of self and world most readily when their survival, and that of their families, depends upon the care of livestock and the seasonally regulated cultivation of the soil. They discover the significance of property—individual or communal, as the case may be—where life is directly dependent upon the right to enjoy what are literally the fruits of one's labor. Pointing out that the Sumerian word *mas* means both "interest" and "newborn animal," Gehlen observes that:

> The notion of capital, of a property which gains in value and demands to be put to use . . . appears within the agricultural economy. . . . Here capital formation is, as it were, an ontological process, a reality within the very substance of life in the world, with its economic significance and its ethical legitimation. Thus there can arise no generalized doubt concerning the rights of property, but, at most, specific objections concerning specific rights. The sacredness of private property constitutes one of the key features of agrarian societies; it delineates the sphere of one's will and power, and the sphere of one's moral responsibility for the prosperity of living things. This total acceptance of the notion of property, as well as the hankering toward stability, the thinking in terms of seasons, years, and generations, and finally the willingness to submit to something conceived as general and as outside one's influence (a conception not yet found in hunting cultures, and no longer in industrial ones), all these categories are crystallized into the central concept of traditional culture, that of *jural order* (*Rechtsordnung*).[6]

6. Gehlen, *Man in the Age of Technology*, 96.

Thus the concept of law as the personified yet impersonal arbiter between already existing rights and interests—a concept central to what we mean by civilized life—arises almost naturally within agrarian societies. So too does the state, conceived as the guarantor of law within and defense without. A settled society, concerned with the care and cultivation of its environment, knows that it can survive only so long as it is endowed with the institutional means of preserving itself against the breakdown of internal order and the threat of external invasion and conquest. In part, such threatening possibilities are prevented by the existence of habits of communal cooperation and regulation that come naturally to those who, out of necessity more than out of choice, share a land and a way of life; but there is also need for an institution, the state, which specializes in such matters and which can, when circumstances demand it, mobilize the resources of the whole society for the defense of its well-being. In agrarian societies, the misdeeds of unjust rulers are a constant cause for complaint, but the need for rulership itself is not called into question any more than is the need for property.

Given the brevity of the period for which even the best-established of the postagrarian societies of the modern world have existed, it is obvious that the origins of their institutions lie in their agrarian past. Hardly less obvious is the observation that the sort of changes that have come about in the way of life of so much of the world over the last century or so could not have occurred without causing considerable disruption at the social-psychological level. Well-established structures of thought and patterns of meaning, which originated in the attempt to make sense of a life overwhelmingly conditioned by the immediacy of its dependence on the tending of soil and livestock, are brought into question when the way of life changes. The self-evidence of the imperatives of political order vanishes when the world that first testified to their necessity is no longer the world one experiences. Since it is in terms of such symbolic patterns, amounting to a total world-view, that men understand their nature and condition, the effect of this change is to produce what one can only call a crisis in human self-identity.

There exists a whole literature, pre-eminently exemplified in the work of Emile Durkheim, in which this crisis is explained as an aspect of the transition from one sort of secure society to another equally secure—from an agrarian society held together by moral bonds founded in an identity of life-style, called by Durkheim "mechanical solidarity," to an industrial society in which there is an "organic solidarity" between individuals who depend upon each other precisely because each is a specialist in only one field of endeavor.[7] This view—that the crisis of modernity is merely a problem of transition between equivalent orders—was always, quite predictably, rejected by the conservative political defenders of the old order. They tended to argue, as Charles Maurras put it, that while there had been an old order there was no new one. Instead, modernity was characterized by the prevalence of conditions that prevented a stable political order from emerging. More recently, the sociological study of the social and cultural processes associated with modernization, as practiced by Peter Berger and his collaborators, has tended to support this view that the fundamental problem of modernity involves more than transition. The problem is not that there is a time-lag in the adaptation of human consciousness to a new situation—a problem that might be solved, as Durkheim supposed, by the creation of a new morality—but that the characteristic self-interpretation of modern man is radically flawed in a way that makes the attainment of a humanly satisfactory political order all but impossible.

Berger finds evidence for this in the fact that, both in the ambitious but technologically backward countries of the Third World and in the already industrialized nations, so much is expected from political institutions by men who are at the same time profoundly impatient with the restraints that the institutions impose. Moral perplexity in the face of changes that are earnestly desired and yet are experienced as utterly disorienting finds political expression in the creation of synthetic ideologies that combine modernizing with antimodernizing themes. The unstable mixture that results from the combination of incompatible aspirations is typically

7. This optimistic argument is to be found in Emile Durkheim, *The Division of Labor in Society*, trans. George Simpson (New York, 1933). For the less sanguine view held by Durkheim later in his life, see "The Dualism of Human Nature," in Emile Durkheim, *Essays on Sociology and Philosophy*, ed. Kurt H. Wolff (New York, 1964).

given a certain plausibility by the use of the rhetoric of "socialism"—a portmanteau term that carries within itself little more
than the promise of the benefits of modernization without its at-
tendant discontents.[8]

The truth is that the fruits of modernization cannot satisfy the
aspirations of modernity, which conceives technological progress
not as a limited and morally ambivalent extension of a primordial
human endeavor but as an adjunct to the magical politics of ontological metastasis. Those who talk unthinkingly of the magic of
modern technology speak more truly than they realize, for just as
once the spells of the sorcerer provided a supernatural technology
intended to overcome the limits of nature, so now a wholly natural
technology is expected to bring man to the supernatural state of
unconditioned being.

We need not attribute the aspirations of modernity to some
inexplicable fall from philosophical grace. We are neither less nor
more natively wise than our ancestors, but the changes we have
wrought in our environment make certain truths less obvious than
once they were. Just as the life-style of the primeval hunter encouraged belief in dependence on the technology of magic, so ours
promotes reliance on the magic of technology. Between the age
of the hunter and our own stands the agrarian era, whose mode of
existence produced an overwhelming impression of the dependence of man—a responsible and careful agent—upon an objective
order attested by the fruitfulness and regularity of nature. The consciousness of that age was not magical but religious.

The problem of modernity is, therefore, not just a hiccup in the
process of modernization. It is rooted in an environmentally influenced transformation of consciousness that does not merely alter but, in a crucial way summed up in the image of the eclipse of
fate, falsifies human self-understanding. It must be stressed that
the change in the nature of man's relationship to the world that

8. This theme is developed with vivid illustrations in Peter L. Berger, Brigitte
Berger, and Hansfried Kellner, *The Homeless Mind: Modernization and Conscious-
ness* (New York, 1973), and Peter L. Berger, *Pyramids of Sacrifice: Political Ethics
and Social Change* (New York, 1974). For Berger's understanding of socialism, see
Peter L. Berger, "The Socialist Myth" and "Toward a Critique of Modernity" in Peter
L. Berger, *Facing Up to Modernity: Excursions in Society, Politics, Religion* (New
York, 1977).

provokes this change of consciousness is real enough. The eclipse of fate designates a state of human misunderstanding that is powerful and pervasive precisely because the experience that underlies it is the experience of a real transformation in man's way of life, which is the result of a genuine alteration in the balance between the ingenious power of the human agent and the formerly implacable power of nonhuman nature. As a phenomenon of modern consciousness, the eclipse of fate occurs because the bounds of fate have undeniably been pushed back to the point at which our everyday experience has become crammed to capacity with the material evidence of a man-made world. Where once man's perspective on the world dictated that he should see it as suffused with life, now it tempts him to regard the world as the quasi-passive matter on which any desired form may be imposed.[9] But if primitive panvitalism was a delusion, so is its modern equivalent. The eclipse of fate is no less delusory for being an almost inevitable consequence of the modern, technologically insulated way of life.

By insulating man from the evidence of his dependence upon necessities that are beyond his power to alter, the technology of the modern world leads him to forget the significance of his finitude. Because technology leads man to believe that in the field of human action all is possible, it tends to encourage an attitude toward mundane political existence that is subversive of the necessary supports and expressions of human social life. Of course, the older view of things also had its typical illusions. In particular, the constant, recurring pattern of agricultural labor—the discipline that is the condition of survival in an agrarian society—encouraged an overestimation of the changelessness of cultural realities. It is not only Marxists—who have a vested revolutionary interest in exposing such "mystifications"—who have noticed the way in which premodern man "ontologizes" his institutions by imagining them to be divinely instituted and cosmologically necessary. In agrarian societies, political institutions are indeed perceived as an integral part of an unchangeable condition to which man is fated. The distinction between the sphere of nature and that of culture seems all

9. This theme runs through the work of Hans Jonas. See especially Hans Jonas, *The Phenomenon of Life: Toward a Philosophical Biology* (New York, 1966), and Jonas, *The Imperative of Responsibility*.

but nonexistent in the context of a generalized consciousness of participation in a single divine order. Yet the very lack of differentiation that seems to make this older view theoretically untenable has its compensations at the level of political practice. If not true, the old order was at least respectful of reality.

In terms of its ontology, the premodern world-view embodied a recognition of the real links that bind the nature of human order to the order of nonhuman nature. Even if, in doing so, it tended constantly to blur the distinction between the two spheres, this was a less dangerous mistake than the typically modern error of supposing that because man constructs certain realities therefore he may reconstruct them as the mood takes him. At the level of anthropology, premodern man, beset on all sides by the evidence of his dependence, could hardly fail to recognize his finitude. He therefore invested his hopes for release from the bounds of earthly existence and for attainment of a state of unconditioned being in a world other than that which must certainly have frustrated them. Moreover, in terms of social psychology the perceived stability of the institutional framework and its self-interpretation provided a secure background of taken-for-granted reality. And this, as Alfred Schutz showed in *The Phenomenology of the Social World*, is the essential precondition for all effective action in the world.[10] No one can act if the premises of action are called repeatedly into question, and it is a vital function of society to provide the individual with the interpretative schemes and initial expectations with which he may approach the open adventure of his life. Those who condemn the tendency of past, or present, societies to "ontologize" or "reify" their institutions by investing them with the dignity of the ontologically given ignore the fact that such a stabilization of worldview in a coherent form that can be shared by the members of society is not merely a psychological comfort but an anthropological necessity on which both interpersonal communication and individual motivation depend.[11]

But in the modern world, man's view of the status of political institutions has become de-ontologized. Just as the old view of

10. Alfred Schutz, *The Phenomenology of the Social World*, trans. George Walsh and Frederick Lehnert (Evanston, Ill., 1967).
11. This is well argued by Burke C. Thomason in *Making Sense of Reification: Alfred Schutz and Constructionist Theory* (London, 1982).

things was consistent with a generalized sense of participation in a world whose form depended on forces beyond human control, so the new expresses the triumph of a view that seeks the submission of the world's order to the requirements of human will. The novelty of this situation lies not in the quest for human mastery as such, but in the fact that the progress of technology has encouraged the belief that mastery can be total. In this perspective, every tension in human existence, including those simple registrations of the fact of finitude that are constitutive of the form of man's being, are perceived as removable frustrations of the course of the will. Modern man is above all impatient with the irremovable facts of life, including the need for the authoritative regulation of life by political institutions.

In contrast to our ancestors, we see only too clearly that political institutions are humanly created realities, justified only by the services they render to those who live subject to them. Regarded thus, institutions have ceased to be part of the taken-for-granted reality of life, persisting, like the needs they serve, unchanged over generations. They are seen instead as tools in the service of particular projects—human artifacts to be modified or laid aside as circumstances change under the impact of our endeavors.

As Berger has put it:

> Archaic institutions are highly objective; that is, they are experienced as inevitable, to-be-relied-upon facts, analogous to the facts of nature. Modern institutions, by contrast, are deficient in this objectivity. They are readily seen and indeed experienced as *ad hoc* constructions, here now and possibly gone tomorrow, in any case not to be taken for granted and always open to radical change. The modern organization is the typical form of this greatly attenuated institution. . . . Another way of describing this process is to say that modernity greatly shrinks the background of human life and correspondingly expands the foreground. Thus modernity is characterized by constant innovation, rationality, and reflectivity, and by a corresponding sense of the unreliability of all social order. This transformation . . . is not just something taking place externally, outside the consciousness of individuals. It also affects consciousness, and vitally so. The reason for this is made clear by Gehlen's philosophical anthropology; while modernity has greatly changed man's social en-

vironment, it has not changed his nature. The same biological species of *Homo sapiens* exists and must come to terms with the new environment. That, however, is very difficult. For man continues to be instinctually deprived, in need of stability and of reliable guide-posts for action. If this stability cannot be produced for him by society, he must somehow seek it within his own consciousness.[12]

Modernity imposes utterly new tensions on man, tensions that are especially discomforting because the being who must live with them is ill-prepared to put up with any tension at all. Of course, at the physical level the advance of technology has made life more secure, at least on a day-to-day basis. But the extension of technological modes of thought to politics involves an unceasing evaluation of institutions in means/end terms. The legitimacy of modern institutions is always provisional and subject to withdrawal by those whose immediate aspirations have not been met. Man is thus deprived of the security of living in a world he can take for granted. Awareness that the form of institutions is not an inevitable consequence of an unchangeable state of being makes him impatient with the restraints the institutions continue to impose. Institutions have ceased to be experienced as extensions to an ontologically comprehended self—a self that understands itself as fated to a certain condition and recognizes its identity to consist in membership of the community in which, without choice, it finds itself. Instead, institutions have come to be seen as mere tools in the service of a restless political will that increasingly has subsumed within its aspirations all the hopes once vested in religion.

One cannot emphasize too strongly that this transformation of political consciousness poses something more than an intellectual problem. It cannot be understood as only the latest chapter in an existentially detached history of ideas. The change is an integral and, in some ways, a quasi-inevitable part of the process by which man has extended his empire over the world in which he continues to dwell. This success in achieving mastery over his immediate environment by technological means makes the technological view of politics superficially credible. In turn, the extension of technological modes of thought to political order promotes a view

12. Peter L. Berger, Foreword to Gehlen, *Man in the Age of Technology*, xi–xii.

of politics as a field of transformative action—*techne* rather than *praxis*—and this opens the way to the temptations of revolutionary ideology.

To those who have read the work of Jürgen Habermas, this will seem a curious argument. Habermas, the most subtle of neo-Marxist social critics, has argued that the technological concept of politics, far from promoting the unrealistic demands of utopian revolution, precludes the pursuit even of attainable emancipatory goals. Our society, he argues, is less free than it might be precisely because, by conceiving political practice as analogous to technology, we confine ourselves to the fine-tuning of an intrinsically flawed system. Recognition of the proper nature of political *praxis* as a system of interhuman communication unrestricted by the constraints imposed by the existence of unequal power relations, rather than as a matter of "technological" manipulation, would lead us to understand the ultimate incompatibility between such *praxis* and the existence of capitalist property relations. Habermas has provided a forceful critique of what he calls the "imitation substantiality" of Gehlen's institutionalism, arguing that Gehlen's obsession with the anthropological imperative of institutionalization prevents him from seeing the possibility that there might exist a form of human association based not upon unthinking conformity to inherited ways, but on collective decisions reached by rational debate between equals. Such a form of association, Habermas argues, is implicit in the very form of communicative discourse.

When human beings communicate with each other through language—which Habermas revealingly calls an "anti-institution"[13]—they anticipate what he calls the "ideal speech situation" in which unrestricted communication could occur. The argument, which Habermas has elaborated at considerable length, runs thus. Communication between men is carried out through language. Linguistic communication only fulfills its inherent function when the intended meaning of the communication is in fact conveyed. Thus the more transparent language is, the more fully it is achiev-

13. "Discourse is no institution at all, it is the anti-institution as such." Jürgen Habermas, *Theorie der Gesellschaft oder Sozialtechnologie*, cited by Henning Ottmann in "Cognitive Interests and Self-Reflection," in James B. Thompson and David Held (eds.), *Habermas: Critical Debates* (London, 1982), 87.

ing its anthropological purpose. But where power relations between potential communicants are unequal, the flow of free communication is disturbed and even broken. We do not talk freely except to our equals. Habermas seems to have adopted the Aristotelian distinction between *praxis* and *techne* from his reading of the work of Hannah Arendt. Arendt's identification of the proper meaning of political life with the life of the Greek *polis* incorporates the classical insight into the foundation of political order in the association of like-minded citizens. The like-mindedness in question is achieved in the freedom of political debate. The specifically Marxist element in Habermas' picture, which goes well beyond Arendt's own strictures on the ethnic and sexual limitations of the Greek conception of citizenship, lies in his view that such debate cannot in fact occur where differential property relations render the participants unequal.

To Habermas, the restraints that institutions place upon men are, except in so far as they are the result of a form of communication that has never yet been possible, equivalent to the compulsive repetitions of neurotic behavior. What Gehlen regards as social health is described by Habermas as the social equivalent of a disease. And just as neuroses can be revealed and overcome by a psychoanalysis that sees them for the disturbances they are, so the legitimation of authoritative institutions can be subjected to a critique of ideology that will show up the gap between what the institutions are and what they pretend to be. This critique, which extends to the attempt to justify institutions on the grounds of a supposedly constant philosophical anthropology, bears witness to what Henning Ottmann has described as Habermas' overestimate of the competence of rational reflection and his corresponding downgrading of the human value of what has already been achieved in political culture.[14]

To regard institutions as the political equivalents of neurotic compulsions, as Habermas does, is to dismiss in an unjustifiably high-handed way the anthropological case for the necessity of a taken-for-granted reality as a precondition for the possibility of all human activity. Looked at from the perspective of philosophical

14. Ottmann, "Cognitive Interests and Self-Reflection," 87.

anthropology, Habermas' so-called critique of ideology is bound to appear as another variation on the ideological fantasy of a post-political world. The "ideal speech situation" that Habermas envisages and by whose transcendental standard he finds the appeal to the authority of institutions unjustifiable is not within the range of political possibility. The existence of a taken-for-granted world is, we must recall, not only a psychological requirement but the precondition for that very communication in which Habermas finds his supposedly objective critical standard. At first glance, the "ideal speech situation" of undistorted communication seems to involve a model of social life based upon the idea that political order is rationally justifiable only to the extent that it resembles a neverending university seminar. A second glance reveals that the analogy with scholarly discussion is more than a little misleading, for in the universal seminar of emancipated existence the demands of critique and unceasing reflection have been extended to such a point that nothing is taken for granted. If there are no indisputable premises for argument, discussion and so communication itself must break down. Unrestricted communication in Habermas' sense would result in no communication at all, for where there is nothing unquestionably common the linguistic community on which the possibility of communication rests will tend to fall apart. As an example of what this means, consider the way in which the efforts of radical feminists to purge the language of emblems of "sexist" domination and male authority have made it impossible for them to debate with their opponents in a common tongue. Wittgenstein argued that a private language was a logical impossibility, but nothing except the authority of linguistic tradition and its transmission over generations by institutions like the family and the school stands in the way of the breakdown of language into a babel of mutually incomprehensible jargons. It is cold comfort to note that such an outcome seems unlikely in the near future, mainly because of the centripetal force of a linguistic standardization impressed on receptive minds by immersion in endless torrents of teletalk.

The impression that Habermas' critical theory is vitiated by a failure to admit to the necessary conditions of human cultural existence is confirmed by his tendency, in his long-running debate with Hans-Georg Gadamer, to regard interpretative traditions and authority as negative influences in man's attempt to understand himself through the appropriation of his past. For his part, Gadamer maintains the indispensibility of authority and tradition against what he provocatively calls the post-Enlightenment "prejudice against prejudice"—a prejudice to which Habermas is heir.

If the language of Habermas, the most liberal of Marxists, echoes the rationalist dream of the eighteenth-century Enlightenment with its refusal to accept the validity of any institution that cannot establish its credentials in terms of reason alone, Gadamer's vocabulary testifies to the influence of Burke and his disciples in the German historical school. And while Habermas trusts in the ultimate power of substantive reason to conjure the form of a new and freer community out of the debate of equals, Gadamer vindicates the authority of tradition, whose pre-judgments or prejudices are always questionable in particulars but can never be rejected in entirety. Gadamer points out that it was only in the course of the eighteenth century that the term *prejudice* acquired its present, generally negative connotation. Originally, prejudice meant not a false judgment incapable of justification but simply "a judgment that is given before all the elements that determine a situation have been finally examined."[15] Prejudice in this sense is not the enemy of true understanding but its necessary first form and even its guide. Not only do we, as a matter of fact, derive most of our knowledge of the world from the society into which we are born without submitting the validity of its testament to lengthy personal examination, but without the guidance of the prior judgment of others—what Schutz called "the stock of knowledge at hand"—we would be utterly unprepared for the circumstances of existence.

In Gadamer's words, "history does not belong to us, but we belong to it. Long before we understand ourselves through the process of self-examination, we understand ourselves in a self-evident way in the family, society and state in which we live. The focus of subjectivity is a distorting mirror. The self-awareness of the individual is only a flickering in the closed circuits of historical life. That is

15. Hans-Georg Gadamer, *Truth and Method*, trans. William Glen-Doepel (London, 1975), 240.

why the prejudices of the individual, far more than his judgements, constitute the historical reality of his being."[16] Wisdom does not consist in attempting to rid ourselves of all such prejudgments, but in allowing the evidence of unfolding experience to modify, where necessary, the prejudices with which, as inexperienced newcomers to the life of a communicative species, we inevitably start.

Against the illusory autonomy of a subjectivity purged of all presuppositions and able to grasp absolute knowledge through the use of reason alone—the dream of Enlightenment philosophy, renewed in more sober guise in the social and socialist myth of "the ideal speech situation"—Gadamer sets the reality of a historically conditioned participatory consciousness. It should be noted that when he emphasizes the historically formed horizon of consciousness as a constant feature in the life of the species, he is not replacing ontology with the philosophy of history in the manner of nineteenth-century Hegelians of Left and Right. Rather, his point is that both the historical moment and the human consciousness that attempts to comprehend it, presently from within or retrospectively from without, are determinations of an ontologically given finitude. "The overcoming of all prejudices," he writes, "this global demand of the enlightenment, will prove itself a prejudice, whose removal opens the way to an appropriate understanding of our finitude, which dominates not only our humanity, but also our historical consciousness."[17]

In thus placing the recognition of finitude at the center of his conception of the human sciences, Gadamer's work represents an important advance in the self-understanding of those distinctively modern enterprises. It is wholly consistent with our understanding of the anthropological insufficiencies of the modern world-view that this advance should consist so largely in the reinstatement of a truth that premodern man could hardly have doubted. The ancient myth of a single, immutable, natural order encompassing nature and society alike provided a general, comprehensible way of expressing a truth that, under modern conditions, can be retrieved only after a laborious trek along the byways of philosophical anthropology and the human sciences. While the undifferentiated on-

16. *Ibid.*, 245.
17. *Ibid.*, 244.

tology that regarded natural and social phenomena as equally objective emanations of a single cosmological scheme can be faulted, it did at least embody a true insight into the necessary conditions of man's participation in being more securely than is even possible today. The rediscovery of the meaning of finitude, which Gadamer's work exemplifies, and with it the vindication of political order against the impossible demands of ideology are two of the most necessary and yet among the most difficult tasks of modern man. No longer self-evident, these truths must now be established by argument, and however well-founded the argument may be, it will always seem tenuous and open to plausible doubt in comparison with the massive testimony to dependence that the whole world once offered to the inhabitant of agrarian society. This too is an aspect of the problem of modernity. The illusion of unconditioned autonomy is, as it were, ingrained in the reality of modern life.

While the premodern consciousness of agrarian communities reflected the experience of a being subject in an obvious way to the demands of the world, modern consciousness typically experiences the world as already subject to human control. Modern man does not therefore feel called upon to conform to an objective order, even though subconsciously he may still feel the need to do so. In so far as he experiences the world as actually possessing an order to which he must conform, he sees the source of that order as lying in nothing beyond the willful and self-interested power of other men. Therefore, if the world is not to his liking, someone must be to blame. The objectivity of world-order is, according to the wisdom of modernity, nothing more than the result of the dominion of others. In this way, by a process of extension, even the accidents of nature come to be seen as subject to the demands of an ill-defined but all-encompassing "social justice." In his recent work, F. A. Hayek has provided an incomparable analysis of the emptiness of such a notion as well as of the harm to which its apparent plausibility leads in the conduct of our social and economic affairs.[18] For present purposes, it is enough to note that the emergence of such a notion is inevitable once men begin to conceive the

18. F. A. Hayek, *The Mirage of Social Justice* (London, 1976). Vol. II of *Law, Legislation, and Liberty*, 3 vols.

world as subject to the demands of a subjectivity which recognizes no independent measure.

Since modern man is quite right to suppose that institutions are in fact human creations, any change in his conception of political order leads to a change in the nature of the institutions that compose it. Subject to the demands of modern consciousness, institutions are transformed increasingly into specialized organizations, charged only with carrying out specified tasks. Each organization is, in principle, distinct from every other. Together or apart, they offer no coherent interpretation of the world, and so, while remaining functionally necessary, they come to seem accidental to the identity of the individual. Here we encounter what may be called the paradox of functionality. It can be stated thus: the greater the functional specialization of a society's institutions, the less well can they fulfill the original and still fundamental anthropological function of institutionalization, which is to provide a stable and intelligible order for human existence.

The institutions of premodern society presented its inhabitants with a coherent model or image of man. Personal identity was acquired through participation in the common life of communities of birth, family and clan, church, and nation. The character of the mature adult was formed through participation in the life of the group and was prized in so far as it was seen to represent the socially shared ideal of manhood. Personal identity was, as it were, an extension of the same factors that held the society together as a cultural unit. At the same time, because the institutions of society were taken for granted, they were experienced positively as agencies of the self who acted through them in concert with his fellows. This situation, in which institutions were recognized as serving the interests of those who lived subject to them, did not have the subjectivist implications of the modern instrumental view. Since in the premodern world the self did not conceive of the possibility of life apart from the institutions in terms of which he comprehended his identity, institutions came to partake of the objective reality of the ontologically given conditions of existence.

Thomas Luckmann—who, like Berger, is a sociologist influenced both by the social phenomenology of Schutz and by Gehlen's philosophical anthropology—has pointed out that, though classical political philosophy and modern social theory agree about the indispensibility of institutions in the ordering of human life and the formation of personal identity, the transformation of institutions into specialized organizations makes it all but impossible for them to answer these requirements.

> The specialization of institutional systems, the weakening or severing of subjectively meaningful ties between experiences and actions which are determined by these systems, the growing anonymity of many social roles, the break between primary and secondary socialization; all these circumstances combine to form a rather new type of socio-historical *a priori* for human organisms that happen to be born now rather than 400, 4,000, or 40,000 years ago. The construction of personal identity has become entrusted to an "institution" which, by its very nature, is *not* an institution, the individual subject.[19]

Thrown back on the insufficiencies of his own resources, deprived of the security of an unquestioned and all-but-unquestionable interpretation of existence shared with his fellows—what Berger and Luckmann call a "symbolic universe" in which every being has an assured place and an intelligible destiny—it is small wonder that the modern individual should be vulnerable to the appeal of ideologies that promise deliverance from the uncertainties and frustrations of mundane existence. Ideology offers the man of today renewed certainty in a form that confirms the technological prejudice of modern consciousness. It reduces the mysteries of human existence to soluble problems of social and economic organization. It promises a world without frustration, conflict, or despair and proposes to achieve such a world by means of the insatiable politics of revolution. However often experience confirms the frightful consequences of such projects, the ideological temptation remains a permanent threat to the stability of modern political order—a constantly renewed threat that no amount of material prosperity can ever entirely banish.

19. Thomas Luckmann, "Personal Identity as an Evolutionary and Historical Problem," in Thomas Luckmann, *Life-World and Social Realities* (London, 1983), 109.

being except by human care; and therefore no institutional order, however securely it may seem to be established, can ever attain the degree of ontological security that characterizes those systems of genetically determined behavioral guidance that impose a specific uniformity on every other type of animal society. In comparison with the organically founded orders of animal societies, political order is always a fragile achievement.

To this perspective on the problem of politics, derived in large part from consideration of Arnold Gehlen's philosophical anthropology and theory of institutions, we must add another to which Eric Voegelin in particular has drawn our attention. An institutional order does not spring up as an automatic response to a perceived need. It must be created and maintained by consciously directed action. Thus the form of society that exists and can exist at any point in history depends crucially on the way in which the men of the time understand their nature and place relative to the world in which they are fated to live. The order of politics reflects the order of consciousness and self-interpretation, and the human consciousness of the historically effective actor is the ordering center that imposes form on human society. Any disorder at the level of consciousness, any misunderstanding of either the ontological or the historical possibilities of action, or any attempt to shift responsibility for order away from consciousness and onto the supposed imperatives of nature or history will have their effects at the level of political life. In politics, the attempt to justify particular actions or policies by appeal to either natural or historical imperatives, in the manner typical of the totalitarian ideologies of our century, is not an answer to a political problem but an attempt to evade the responsibility for the ordering of his life that is man's fate. Human action as a whole, including the action required for the maintenance of the conditions favorable to the good life, is always a response to the given natural and historical state of the world; but the form the response takes, the activity that sustains the human world in being, cannot be guided by anything but the rational considerations of consciousness. It is, as Aristotle saw, not history or nature but the practical wisdom of the mature and well-informed man that alone can determine the appropriate political form of the good society. Political thought and political practice are two aspects of a single project—the unending project of imagining and realizing the form of life most favorable to the actualization of the highest possibilities of human existence.

There is therefore a dual imperative, known to reason, that runs through the political project. At every time and place, man is faced with the need to order his social existence in a way that allows him to survive in the world. But organic survival is not enough. In the construction of political order, man does not seek merely to erect a shelter against the pressures of a potentially threatening environment. He seeks to attune his existence to what he understands to be the true order of his being. It is not sufficient to live, though the preservation of life is the precondition for everything else; what is required is to live in truth, in loving response to the demands of the Being that gives one life. In archaic societies and in what Voegelin calls cosmological civilization, the order of being is identified with the sustaining order of the cosmos, regarded and revered as itself divine. Following the epochal events that Voegelin describes in Bergsonian terms as "leaps in being," the measure of order and source of truth are rediscovered in the revelation of a world-transcendent God. The immediate, mundane transcendence of the cosmos as the commanding measure of man is displaced by the ultimate transcendent authority of One on Whom even the existence of the cosmic order of the universe depends. In his studies of Greek philosophy, Voegelin has shown that this displacement of the authority of the cosmos—a quasi-natural though superhuman authority that modern naturalistic anthropologies have sought to revive, though in a new disguise—is inevitable if consciousness is allowed to pursue unhindered the question of its own origin and foundation.

It says nothing against the epochal significance of the leap in being to note that, in both the cosmological symbolization of order and the revelatory and philosophical ones, man, recognizing his dependence on an order of being beyond his control, seeks to order his life through attunement to whatever he conceives to be the demands of that order. In contrast to the typical self-understanding of man today, the purpose of existence is not seen as the pursuit of the satisfaction of unmeasured material and emotional desires but as the effort to approximate the form of one's life as closely as possible to the demands of a given and unalterable state of being. Human life is conceived in terms less of expression than of response.

It is in the eclipse of this once deeply rooted and all-but-universal interpretation of the human condition that what I shall call the new problem of politics arises. As I see it, the gravity of the problem lies in the fact that the same technologically induced changes that eroded the experiential ground of the older conception have created a situation in which not only the existence of particular humanly valuable forms of political order but, at the limit, the very survival of the species is put at risk. The moral and institutional resources that could guard us against the dangers of political conquest and regression to a lower form of social existence are weakened by the same tendencies in history that have brought us to the point at which the survival of the earth has become a matter for human decision. What in the last chapter I called the "technological view of politics" is eroding the social-psychological foundation of the stability of Western institutions. The ground is slipping beneath the statesmen's feet at a time when the development of technology itself, in the civil as well as the military sphere, is making the task of statesmanship more vital than ever before.

Historically speaking, there is then a new problem of politics. We still need the humanized world embodied in institutional order, and the creation and maintenance of such a world remains the essential task of politics—that is always the fundamental problem. The novelty of our situation lies in the fact that in the modern world the difficulty of this task has been magnified by factors that both raise the stakes at issue in the project and diminish the chance that an institutional order that is both politically effective and humanly—psychologically and morally—satisfying can be sustained. Where the natural world that supports human life is subject to the dispensations of man's untrammeled technological power, nature itself becomes a quasi-institution—a structure vulnerable to the same inherently unrestrained ambitions and cares that have always made even the best of political achievements fragile. In this situation, the very possibility of human survival is for the first time put at political risk—and this at a moment when the restraining power of institutional authority, formerly sustained by an awareness of human finitude born of the experience of dependence on a world-order beyond wilful control, has been weakened by the eclipse of fate induced by our apparent success in mastering the immediate environment.

To the ontologically given problem of politics, which is coeval with man, we must therefore add a new complex of problems that derive from the transformation of the conditions of life accomplished by modernity. By extending the effective range of human agency in time and space, these changes bring a new area within the scope of ethical and political decision. This is the objective dimension of the problem—a fact of life, whether we recognize it or not. But no less significant is the subjective dimension—the extent to which man's self-interpretation is so altered by the apparent subjugation of nature to will that the sense of finitude and the necessity of attuning one's life to a transcendent measure have come to be rejected as marks of servitude to imaginary powers. Without ceasing to live in the world, modern man has lost his cosmic sense of existing in an ontologically given order. In imagination, he lives within and toward what Gehlen has called a "secular horizon"—a stage whose limits are fixed not by the implacable structures of cosmic or divine commands but by the shifting limits of a technological enterprise that recognizes in every encountered limit only the provocation to push a little further.[1]

In drawing attention to the extent to which the new problem of politics—the problem of politics in a technological age—is conditioned by the growth of technology itself, I am not arguing for any variety of technological determinism. I simply note that the growth of technology expands the spatial and temporal range of effective human action, and that this expansion creates a cultural environment in which certain truths about the imperatives of political order tend to be forgotten. But this does not mean that the political problem of modernity is determined in its outcome by the dynamics of modern technology, merely that the novelty of an environment in which so many of the previously implacable limits of existence have been overcome alters man's perspective on an anthropological problem that is, in principle, unchanged. It is not the

1. Arnold Gehlen, *Man in the Age of Technology,* trans. Patricia Lipscomb (New York, 1980), 93–111.

problem that is changed but the conditions under which it must now be approached and answered through the practice of politics. Even this formulation is perhaps an exaggeration. The novelty of the modern technological age is apparent enough, but the dynamic of technological change, though vastly accelerated over the last two centuries, is not an anthropological novelty in itself. The need to develop some form of control over the environment—the original motive of technology—is inscribed in the primordial human condition. In relation to the regulation of human social life, we have spoken at length of the need to create institutions as a substitute for the instinctual guidance that our species lacks. But the deficiencies of man at the level of the human organism are no less apparent when we consider him in relation to his natural environment. In purely organic terms, man is unfitted for survival in the world. The root of technology as well as the root of politics is to be found in this anthropologically fundamental fact.

The development of the primitive technology of tool and weapon production parallels from the beginning the process of institutionalization. In both spheres of endeavor human ingenuity discovers answers to the vital questions encountered in the course of existence. These answers are not ready-made and cannot be called forth from any hidden reserve of genetically transmitted wisdom. They are works of practical reason, and once achieved they are transmitted by cultural means alone. If institutions are man's substitute for the absent guidance of instinct, and tools and weapons the human replacement for the lack of sufficient organic means of sustenance and defense, then tradition, as the means of transmitting acquired solutions from one generation to the next, forms a cultural equivalent to the informing messages of the biologically inherited genetic code. It preserves the identity of the group, but with a responsiveness to change that has no real biological equivalent, for while the genetic code is fixed and cannot, outside the sphere of humanly controlled biological engineering, alter except as a result of chance mutations, tradition as the medium of cultural transmission is responsive to the same sort of consciously recognized pressures that give it content in the first place.

Politics and technology together provide the precondition for human survival and the possibility of self-realization. Technology equips man with the means of assuring his continued survival in ways that his body alone cannot provide. Political order, embodied in authoritative institutions, ensures, however imperfectly, that the increased power that technology affords works to the survival rather than the destruction of the group by regulating the uses to which tools and weapons are put.

The technological project is therefore no less inscribed in the human fate than the project of politics. But in itself technology is never more than a morally neutral means of widening the material possibilities of human existence. Every technological advance extends man's control over his environment, but whether such advances serve a humanly valuable purpose is something technological considerations cannot decide, for the extension of man's dominion over nature, while intrinsically necessary to human survival, is ambivalent in its long-term implications. The same power that expands the possibilities of life can, at the limit, undermine the conditions that make life possible. It is the function of the practical reason manifested in the political project to regulate the uses to which technology is put. The effectiveness of this regulation depends in its turn upon the extent to which the considered judgments of practical reason are embodied in institutions that make sound practice a matter of habit.

The greater the powers of technology, the more vital becomes the necessity of institutional guidance and restraint. But the principles that must govern this guidance cannot be derived from the technological project itself, which aims purely at the extension of man's power to manipulate, control, and transform the environment and is therefore incapable of self-regulation. They must be drawn from that other region of human consideration, the field of ethics and politics, which concerns itself with determining the form of life that best approaches the state in which man feels himself attuned to what he knows to be the true order of his being. In this light, the new problem of politics presents itself in the lack of balance between the unrestrained innovatory dynamic of modern technology and the declining ability of institutions to order the conduct of life. The rationality of the modern de-institutionalized individual, caught up in the pursuit of his own short-term private satisfactions, is no substitute for the collective wisdom that finds expression in the institutions of moral and political life and in the sense of meaning they traditionally embody.

In the last chapter, I attempted to sketch the way in which the development of modernity tends to undermine the stability and authority of institutional order without overcoming the anthropological need for institutions that fulfill both practical and symbolic functions as "world preservers." I suggested that there is a whole range of institutions—private property, the constitutionally delimited state, the rule of law—that arise against the background of a form of life dominated by the imperatives of agricultural production. The relatively unchanging forms of agrarian existence that endure from generation to generation, the dependence of agricultural property upon attunement to the rhythms of nature, the intimate relationship between personal effort and interpersonal cooperation in assuring the means of survival, and the knowledge that the whole enterprise depends upon a politically maintained order that ensures the security of the homestead, produce a view of the world that is profoundly respectful of the imperatives of political life. Reverence toward the requirements of nature is matched by a reverence toward those institutions that permit the conduct of social life to continue undisturbed by humanly induced disorder. Knowledge that survival depends upon attunement to forces ultimately beyond human control also makes agrarian man particularly receptive to a religion which teaches that the true order of life is not to be found in the pursuit of short-term satisfactions, though these certainly have their own subsidiary place, but in obedience to divine command.

With the growth of industrialization, man's sense of dependence upon what is superhuman begins to wither. The rhythms of labor are no longer tied to the seasons but to the humanly imposed requirements of factory production. The agrarian form of the community of labor, which is more often than not identical with the community of the family, is replaced by the experience of working alongside strangers brought together by nothing more than another man's productive projects. The world of urban existence is all too obviously a world created to serve exclusively human purposes. If the industrial laborer finds the conditions of his life unsatisfying, he learns to blame not fate but the selfishness, the ambitions, and the greed of those who now control his life. The form of order comes to be seen as exclusively subject to human will.

At the same time, the dynamism of industrial production does not leave the worker's material conditions untouched. The growth of industry, technological innovation, and the use of a plethora of humanly created materials enable an industrial system to meet many of the worker's newly acquired aspirations. This positive development, however, only confirms the impression that the world, now subject to human control, can be depended upon to answer every need and desire. The psychology of attunement to implacable circumstance withers in the face of rising expectations regularly met by technological innovation.

These developments cannot fail to alter the way in which the political realm and the state in particular are regarded. Traditionally, the role of the state was to ensure order within society by maintaining the rule of law and to provide sufficient defense against potential enemies beyond the borders. To some extent, these imperatives continue to be recognized, though to insist on their primacy over all other governmental functions is popularly regarded as the sign of a political reactionary, for the state today has become an integral part of the machinery of desire. Its authority, no longer perceived as an inevitable complement to human insufficiencies, has come to depend upon its ability to satisfy the material aspirations of its inhabitants. This is a problem for the West in particular.

In the postwar years the political institutions of the Western democracies achieved an unprecedented degree of security. The defeat of Nazi Germany and the diminishing reputation of Soviet-style socialism reduced the appeal of the revolutionary ideologies that had exerted such influence in the economically troubled years between the wars. The new legitimacy afforded by the negative example of the totalitarian empires was reinforced by the experience of a rapidly rising standard of living. If one looks at the development of Western political rhetoric over the twenty-five years that followed the end of World War II, one finds a growing tendency to justify the Western system, not in terms of its political virtues, but by its ability to satisfy the material ambitions of its inhabitants. A new image of the state, projected by politicians and eagerly ac-

cepted by electorates, distracted attention from the essential business of politics. Parties vied with each other in their promises of
increased prosperity. A multitude of specialized welfare agencies
was established. Organizations concerned with education, health,
and what came to be called "social security," financed through
taxation of an expanding economy, were created in order to meet
desires that were, as often as not, magnified by the rhetoric of the
politicians themselves. An increasing proportion of the population
became, in one way or another, pensioners of the state.

Even before the recession, which followed the 1973 rise in oil
prices, began to undermine confidence in the state as a bottomless
honeypot, the revival of extreme left-wing ideologies, especially
among the children of the prosperous middle classes, had raised
doubts about the long-term prospects of a system that based its
legitimacy upon its ability to satisfy material demands. At about
the same time, the rise of the ecology movement, though often in
forms that confused a legitimate emphasis on the need for a balance between man and nature with utopian schemes of social re-
organization, reintroduced to the political agenda the question of
human and natural limitations.

These developments are familiar enough. Taken together, they
have, I believe, altered the cultural context of political practice in
a way that acutely questions the very foundations of political order.
The illusion that political success depends upon the fine-tuning of
a system in whose institutional form the outlines of a humanly
satisfying order have already, once and for all, been established has
been severely dented. The revival of ideology has called into question the ability of liberal democratic systems to command the
allegiance even of those whose material interests they serve best.
The tendency of such systems to legitimize themselves by the
promise to fulfill ever-increasing demands for personal prosperity
and autonomy reveals their inherent weakness when those demands reach a point where they can no longer be satisfied by the
finite possibilities of the economy or within the social imperative
of a common moral order. The work of economists like E. J. Mishan
and philosophers of technology like Hans Jonas tends to show that
the limits to the fulfillment of the sort of desires involved, far from
being removable by another round of fine-tuning, are, at least for

the foreseeable future, absolute.[2] Whatever the eccentricities of certain ecologists—eccentricities that manifest themselves both in an over-pessimistic estimate of the chances for the species' survival and, particularly among the German "Greens," in the absurd supposition that the restrictiveness of the political and economic institutions of capitalism is to blame for our problem—there is a profound truth in the ecological argument that the renewal of a humanly maintained balance between the demands of man and the possibilities of nature is now a central question on the political agenda. The maintenance of such a balance, already endangered by the extension of technology to the point where the countervailing pressure of nature alone is insufficient, is made more difficult by a democratization of politics that makes the legitimacy of leadership dependent on the leaders' ability to satisfy the material desires of the least informed.

In drawing attention to the political significance of the desires of those I call the "least informed," I mean something more than the obvious point that those whose aspirations the politician is required to meet represent the element in the population least likely to take account of the long-term consequences of policy decisions. Such consequences are always uncertain, and there is indeed a great deal to be said for the view that a liberal democratic system, which through the mechanism of regular contested elections places a premium on the satisfaction of short-term aspirations, is very much preferable to any alternative that pretends to possess a knowledge of future circumstances and how they may be met by long-term economic and social planning. F. A. Hayek's account of the complexity of social processes and his consequent critique of the ethos of socialistic planning—a critique based on a demonstration of the inevitable cognitive inadequacy of the data on which plans must be founded—seem to me to be both logically irrefutable and empirically corroborated by the failures of such plans in actual practice.[3]

2. E. J. Mishan, *The Costs of Economic Growth* (London, 1967); Hans Jonas, *The Imperative of Responsibility: In Search of an Ethics for the Technological Age*, trans. Hans Jonas and David Herr (Chicago, 1984).

3. This theme runs through Hayek's *oeuvre*, but see, especially, F. A. Hayek, *The Constitution of Liberty* (London, 1960), and F. A. Hayek, *Law, Legislation, and Liberty* (3 vols.; London, 1982).

Nevertheless, as Hayek has also pointed out, an electorate whose political expectations have been conditioned by the experience of a state that presents and justifies itself as the preeminent fount of material benefit—the creator of an ill-defined condition of "social justice"—is one that is profoundly ill-informed about the functions and possibilities of political institutions. In such conditions, which obtain to a greater or lesser extent in all the Western states, the relationship between the individual and the institutions that continue to exert authority over him is necessarily uneasy, for what the state is primarily expected to do is just what it is least capable of achieving. The institutions of public life are expected to answer directly the private aspirations of the individual citizens. In so far as they fail to do this in the matter of material satisfactions, the citizen experiences them as agencies of pure constraint whose sole purpose is to frustrate those other aspirations that seek fulfillment in the pursuit of sensual pleasure. The disciplines of political existence, no longer conceived as an integral aspect of man's earthly vocation, are experienced as external and barely tolerable curbs upon the aspirations of the "authentic" de-institutionalized self.

In recent years a number of writers, influenced above all by the work of Hannah Arendt, have sought to answer this problem of political alienation by reviving a notion of politics derived from the classic Aristotelian model. The key word for these writers has been *participation.* Their arguments have been variations on the theme that the abiding fault of modern political systems has been the gap that has opened up between a public sphere, increasingly dominated by political "experts," and the private universe of a population that plays no part in policy decisions and is consequently alienated from the political process.

As an example of such work, let us look at the argument advanced by Ronald Beiner in his recent book *Political Judgement.* Rejecting the ideological dismissal of politics as an intrinsically alienating activity, Beiner follows Arendt in arguing for the dignity of politics and the humanizing effect of political activity, properly conceived, on those who participate within it. While Arendt's philosophical approach was predominantly modern in inspiration, influenced by both Kant and Heidegger, her view of politics was authentically classical. She held that the proper conception of poli-

tics was that developed within the city-states, the exemplary polities of classical Greece in which rule was vested in the citizenry as
a whole. It is fitting that Arendt's writing should provide the starting point for a work like Beiner's, which attempts to locate the
essence of politics "not in the phenomena of power or interest or
rule or most of the other concerns that dominate present political life, but . . . in language, deliberation and judgement."⁴ What
Beiner seeks to offer is what he calls "a redefinition of citizenship"
in terms of participation in a sphere of common judgment. Since
judgment is a universal human faculty required at every stage of
life between infancy and senility, his argument aims at the restoration of the classical, specifically Aristotelian sense of politics as
a common human vocation. What he opposes is the modern tendency to view politics as a sphere of specialized decision-making
into which only the "expert" can or should enter. To profess politics, Beiner argues, it is not necessary to be a political professional;
it is enough to be a man possessed of normal human faculties.

Like Arendt and Habermas before him, Beiner attributes present
dissatisfaction with political activity and institutions to the transformation of politics from a sphere of *praxis*, governed by shared
judgments concerning the proper ends of communal life, to one
supposedly governed by purely technical concern with the realization of ends that are presumed by governors and governed alike to
be beyond the rational consideration of the citizen. "Politics removed from the sphere of common judgement," he argues, "is a
perversion of the political, and as such, cannot help but manifest
itself in political crisis."⁵ Beiner's diagnosis of the causes of political disenchantment in Western society, while owing a great deal to
Arendt, is of particular significance in the present context because
of the way in which his examination of the nature, scope, and justification of political judgment draws also upon Gadamer's more
recent vindication of Aristotle's notion of practical philosophy.
The influence of Gadamer, evidenced in Beiner's emphasis upon
the inescapable contingency of political judgments and the forms
of life that result from them, protects him against Arendt's more

---

4. Ronald Beiner, *Political Judgement* (London, 1983), xiv.
5. *Ibid.*, 3.

eccentric conclusions as well as against Habermas' ideologically founded impatience with all existing and hence imperfect orders.

Through the examination of Kant's concept of taste and Aristotle's concept of prudence, Beiner lays the foundation for a theory of political judgment that provides a plausible account of the nature of a satisfactory political existence. Not only are we actually engaged in reaching judgments in the everyday course of life, but close attention to what the practice of judgment involves reveals it to be a rational process founded, in the last resort, in a common human experience of what the world shows itself to be. This may be described either in Kantian or in Aristotelian terms, but either way the significance of emphasizing the lived reality of common experience is that it provides judgment with a measure that claims to transcend the mere appeal to private preference. Political judgment, as Beiner conceives it, is not a matter of identifying particular events as instances of one or another general type. It is, in Kant's terms, a variety of reflective rather than determinant judgment. It involves reflection upon a shared, historically unfolding experience and a grasp of the individual event or predicament as both unique and yet a recognizable part of the common world. Political judgment is not a technique that can be taught but a practice perfected only by experience; and Beiner distinguishes political from other reflective judgments not in a formal sense but by the greater scope of their implications. We are, he argues, always responsible for our political fate, and political judgments are "characterized by implicit judgements about the form of collective life that it is appropriate for a community to pursue."[6] To make such judgments is the prerogative of every rational being, and their shared object is the shared experience of the life-world.

In Beiner's work we can, I believe, recognize an unusually well-considered response to the new problem of politics, one that avoids to a considerable extent the ideologization of Aristotelian practical philosophy that characterizes the work of those numerous authors who have been more influenced by Habermas. He calls in the old world of political discourse to remedy the deficiencies of the new, emphasizing the foundation of political community in a commu-

6. *Ibid.*, 138.

nity of speech and judgment without, like Habermas, making the existence of such a community dependent upon the absence of institutionalized authority. If, as I have argued, human beings are essentially active beings, fated to the construction of a suitable world through political practice in which conscious reflection takes the place of absent instinct, it follows that, as Beiner suggests, this practice must resolve itself in the rational process of political judgment. A society in which people feel themselves cut off from this sphere of judgment—one in which politics is only something that happens to them, a spectacle enacted by others—is experienced as something less than a satisfactory polity.

The revival of the model of the classical participatory polity as an answer to the modern problem of alienation from politics is an attractive suggestion, and it is not surprising that many writers have adopted it in one form or another, though few with Beiner's grasp of what it involves. And yet it seems to me that in the cultural conditions of modernity such a revival stands little chance of success. The difference in scale between ancient and modern polities works against it, as does the extended range of the effects of action to which Hans Jonas has drawn our attention. The first point certainly makes it difficult to envisage the form that effective and rational participation could take; while the second makes it doubtful how far even an informed citizenry could be depended on to exercise its judgment with the necessary degree of prudence.[7]

The analysis of the importance of institutionalization in the economy of human existence and its fate in the conditions of the modern world suggests that the problem is deeper than even these considerations imply. The revival of a neoclassical form of polity depends upon the re-creation of a politically responsible and informed citizenry, but this is just what seems least likely in present circumstances. The sense of responsibility required in sound political judgment involves more than the typically modern desire to have some say in the control of one's life, though this is all that is usually expressed in the common demand for a more participatory form of democracy. The sense of responsibility that politics requires also encompasses the awareness of human finitude—which

7. For a searching inquiry into these issues, see Hans Jonas, *The Imperative of Responsibility.*

in the last chapter I called the sense of fate—that recognizes the limits of human possibilities and respects the necessity of institutionalized authority in a political sphere that is both perfectly necessary and necessarily imperfect.

We may envy an age that could ignore the fundamental problem of politics in the confident assurance that the appropriate institutional framework for the good life—representative institutions and the rule of law—had already been discovered, but it is our particular fate to face the problem anew in full awareness that, whatever the value of established institutions and doctrines, they have become questionable in an environment radically changed by human ingenuity. Not only is every existing institution subject to a restless questioning that cannot be satisfied by any answer that falls short of an unattainable perfection, but in truth we do not even know how far established institutions will prove capable of dealing with the new problems raised by the massive increase in the scope of technology.

The problem of politics today is further exacerbated by the fact that the idea of man as a naturally political animal and of political order as the form of life specifically appropriate to his existence—an idea taken for granted in the Hellenic *polis* and whose classical expression is found in the work of Aristotle—has been widely discredited by influential ideologies. Proponents of these ideologies question the necessity of institutional guidance and constraint and promise a postpolitical world of unlimited freedom and spontaneous community. This undeniably appealing fantasy is based, as I have argued, on a confusion between the hopes of religion and the project of politics—between a supernatural destiny whose true assurance is only to be found in faith and the fate of a finite being implicated in the knowable facts of mundane life. It has been given a veneer of realism by the argument, central to Marxism, that human labor has so transformed man's conditions of existence, and hence his nature, that there is no longer a need for the ordering of life by authoritative institutions.

This idea finds expression in many forms, from Habermas' vision of the "ideal speech situation" to the promised "withering away of the state" that continues to legitimize the tyrannical practice of Soviet socialism. In a recent brilliant book aptly called

Lenin and the End of Politics, A. J. Polan has shown how the totalitarian direction taken by the Soviet state since 1917 is precisely
implied in *The State and Revolution*, where Lenin declares the
apparently libertarian intention of creating a society without state
institutions. The political significance of Polan's analysis is considerable, for it is, of course, the promise of unrestrained freedom
rather than the practice of an unrestrained state that gives the communist ideal its residual appeal among those not yet subject to its
yoke. It is precisely this promise, and the attempt to realize it, that
produces the apparently contradictory practice of totalitarian control in the service of total liberation. An analysis that recognizes
this fact provides an admirable case study of the inhuman implications of the ideological attempt to abolish politics and so attain
the ontologically transformed state of postpolitical existence.[8]

As all this implies, the continuing appeal of ideological fantasies
does not lie in anything that has actually been accomplished in
their name. Rather, as I argued in the last chapter, the fantasy of
postpolitical existence is given whatever credibility it has by the
changed conditions of life in the most technologically advanced
societies, that is, in the liberal-democracies of the West. These are
also the societies that have the most to lose from any increase in
the influence of revolutionary, anti-institutional ideology, for they
are by and large the societies in whose institutional form the bal-

8. Thus, for example, A. P. Sheptulin writes in a recent authoritative manual,
Marxist-Leninist Philosophy, trans. Stanislav Ponomarenko and Alexander Timo-
feyev (Moscow, 1978), 488, "During the socialist revolution effected by the proletariat in alliance with the peasantry and other sections of the working people, capitalism is supplanted by the new socialist mode of production, which represents the
economic basis of the new, *communist* socio-economic system. The communist
socio-economic system is marked by an unprecedentedly high level of development
of the productive forces, capable of ensuring the production of the abundant material wealth required to meet all society's demands. Here, production relations are
associated with the domination of the single communist ownership of the means of
production, the absence of classes and class distinctions and the operation of the
principle from each according to abilities to each according to his needs. The state
will wither away and be replaced by communist self-administration. Law will disappear together with the state. Social intercourse will be regulated by moral norms,
resting on the force of public opinion." For the consequences of trying to achieve
such a state of affairs, see A. J. Polan, *Lenin and the End of Politics* (London, 1984).
For a disenchanted analysis of the system in practice, written from a perspective
that still tries to remain within the bounds of Marxist socialism, see Ferenc Fehér,
Agnes Heller, and György Márkus, *Dictatorship Over Needs* (Oxford, 1983).

ance between the imperatives of political order and the opportunities of individual self-realization is best achieved. However, by
encouraging the illusion that self-realization can flourish in the absence of institutional restraint, the very success of the liberal-
democracies in establishing a clear distinction between the public
and the private sphere leaves them ever open to the siren call of
ideology. In emphasizing the inviolable, quasi-sacral quality of individuality as such, liberal political culture diminishes the moral
claims of the shared political order, on which, nevertheless, the
privileged existence of the private sphere continues to depend.

In liberal-democratic societies, there is a widely perceived gap
between the imperatives of institutional guidance and the aspirations of the citizens whose interests the institutions are supposed
to serve. At first sight, this seems strange, since liberal societies
are precisely those in which the main purpose of the public sphere
of government is conceived in terms of the preservation and, where
possible, the extension of a private sphere removed from regulation
by law or custom. If, as we readily admit, the existence of a private
sphere is essential to what we mean by the good life, if we allow
that the purpose of politics is to assure not merely organic survival
but the greatest possibility of living well, it follows that the liberal
conception of the purpose of government cannot be wholly mistaken. Furthermore, once we have admitted the importance of
assuring the existence of a private sphere of life, it seems obvious
that one measure of the success of a government will be the degree
of autonomy it allows the individual in control over his life and
property. Thus far the liberal reasoning seems faultless, yet there
is within it a hidden implication that needs to be brought out. The
justification of government in terms of the maintenance of the private sphere is faulty not in what it says but rather in respect of
what it leaves unspoken—which is the continuing dependence of
the practice of effective individual autonomy upon a political and
legal framework whose imperatives are those of group survival and
not the potentially disruptive satisfaction of individual aspirations.

The practice of the liberal-democratic state is generally admirable enough, but the moral and political assumptions that it
promotes tend to undermine the possibilities of its continued existence. Between the practice of liberal constitutionalism and the

liberal ethic of the primacy of the individual over the group, there is a tension that threatens the survival of the whole finely balanced structure. The liberal conception of the primacy of individual autonomy over public authority diminishes the sense of political realism by making the legitimacy of institutions, at least in popular perception, dependent upon their efficacy in serving rather than curbing private aspirations. The prime anthropological function of politics in maintaining a common public world of institutional—that is, noninstinctual—order is eclipsed in a social vision that identifies the highest good with the satisfaction of human desires whose very lack of inherent instinctual restraint is the ultimate source of the institutional imperative.

There are at least two distinct autodestructive tendencies within the liberal-democratic order. Both are connected with the identification of its governing ideal with the maximization of individual autonomy. In the first place, the moral primacy accorded to the autonomy of the individual weakens the authority of the very institutions on whose existence the possibility of effectively exercised autonomy depends. Prime among these are the legal institutions that restrain the pursuit of privately satisfying projects wherever these threaten either public order or the legitimate autonomy of others. Where the maximization of individual autonomy is conceived as the highest ideal, the rule of law remains secure only in so far as each individual considers the autonomy of others to be as sacred as his own. This of course is just what Kantian morality tells us we should do, but a society that tends, like ours, to conceive the highest good in terms of material and sensual satisfaction rather than, like Kant, in the fulfillment of a rationally apprehended duty, is hardly likely to be one in which such an imperative is widely respected. The liberal order, and the Kantian morality that is its ethical equivalent and on whose practice its preservation as order rather than as anarchy depends, is itself historically and culturally dependent upon preliberal institutions and on the habits of thought and practice that these encouraged among our forebears, who took them for granted as part of a divinely created cosmic order. Liberal-democratic order therefore can be said to live off a moral and political capital for whose care it has little respect, and the recent elevation of private satisfaction above public duty makes it almost certain that this order is living far beyond its means. The declining respect for politics and the rule of law that we perceive throughout the Western world places at risk the very form of autonomous existence that seeks to extend its independence from institutionalized restraint.

The second way in which the political quest for maximal autonomy tends to destroy the possibility of realizing even part of its ambition is the tendency of liberal individualism to evolve in the direction of collectivist socialism. Between liberalism and what is normally regarded as the socialist project of the welfare state as provider of the citizen's needs from cradle to grave, there is indeed an integral connection, for where political institutions are no longer regarded as the focus of allegiance and the embodiment of cultural identity in a community of fate, they come to be reconceived and so reconstructed as ancillary means in the service of individual desires. The citizen encounters the state not as the necessary vehicle of his struggle to survive as a member of a shared culture with its own distinct and valued identity, but as the dispenser of unconditional benefits whose purpose is to facilitate his private satisfactions.

When we speak of the legitimacy of political leadership in the modern liberal-democratic state as dependent on its ability to satisfy the material and emotional desires of the least informed, it is to a special and somewhat unfamiliar sense of "information" that we are ultimately referring. Returning to the Voegelinian theme of the primacy of self-interpretation in determining the form of social life, at precisely the point where it intersects with Gehlen's diagnosis of the anthropological consequences of de-institutionalization, we see that the structure of human life is a passage from infancy to adulthood conceived as, in large part, a process of information. The human infant passes through the stages of organic development like the young of every other species, but the journey to adulthood, while conditional upon physical, organic development, is not, as in the case of the animal, reducible to it. To become an adult is to realize oneself as a moral and social being through the acquisition of language and the attainment of a socially recognized identity that results from participation in the institutionalized order of the polity.

Let us recall again the words of Hans Jonas: "Man models, experiences, and judges his own inner state and outward conduct after the image of what is man's. Willingly or not he lives the idea of man—in agreement or in conflict, in acceptance or in defiance, with good or with bad conscience. The image of man never leaves him, however much he may wish at times to revert to the bliss of animality. To be created in the image of God means to have to live with the image of man."[9] The human self exists in infancy as mere potential. Its actualization depends upon its subsequent formation through increasingly active participation, at first within the family and then in the wider circles of social life. Receiving information from the surrounding culture, the self is formed within by the prevailing image of man and his condition. The informed adult is not merely an organically mature example of man who possesses the information made available to him by his society; the essence of his self-hood, the core of his identity, is formed and articulated within through appropriation and absorption of a cultural heritage which, as much as his genetic inheritance, makes him what he is. The information of the adult citizen, on whose participation the polity depends, is ordered by the cultural in-formation in which the passage to maturity consists.

In anything more than the biological sense, human identity is not a given fact but a lifelong quest that achieves itself in culturally specific forms. What I seek to be in the course of life is modeled after the image of manhood that I discover in the life-world about me. The possible existence of any particular form of polity depends, therefore, on the type of adult who is available to maintain it. This is an insight central to the thought of both Plato and Aristotle, but it is obscured by the modern liberal theory of socialization, which overestimates the possibilities of formal moral and civic education within a society where the inseparability of human fulfillment and institutional restraint is no longer taken for granted.

No one who compares the image of manhood that prevailed in the *polis* during the brief period of its flourishing with that prevailing today can fail to notice the difference. In Aristotle's day, the image, and with it the political order it once sustained, had already

9. Hans Jonas, *The Phenomenon of Life: Toward a Philosophical Biology* (New York, 1966), 185–86.

decayed. Like Aristotle, we can appreciate it as a noble and humanly possible ideal, but not as one that can be realized in all historical circumstances. The same prevalence of private aspirations
over public duty and communal allegiance—the decline of the political ethic of reciprocal obligation between man and institution,
citizen and state—that undermined the independence of the Greek
cities is, in the modern world, erected into a moral ideal. And today, just as then, there are great despotic powers ready to take advantage of this fact to extend their dominion over the world.

The moral formation of the typical modern individual does little
to prepare him for the authentically political life of reciprocal obligation on which the classical participatory polity relied. He experiences his passage to adulthood as a progressive emancipation
from the control of the only sort of institution he knows—the
family and, in Gehlen's terms, the quasi-familiar institutions
which, through infancy and childhood, support him within a
framework of nonreciprocal obligation and responsibility. Infancy
is a state of immediate and unreasoned desires, and of helplessness
whose deficiencies are met by the family in accord with a morality
as natural and universal as anything in the human world can be.
But this is not the ethic that sustains political order, and, as
Gehlen points out, the extension of the familial ethic of one-way
moral obligation from infancy into the adult world of politics has
fatal implications. It is, he argues, just such an extension that characterizes the evolution of modern liberal societies. The culture of
modernity greatly extends the period of childhood, and throughout
that formative period a quasi-familial, nonreciprocal ethic governs
the relationship between the future citizen and the institutionalized world. The child demands, the institution supplies. In the process, an increasingly differentiated and rationalized range of desires
continues to be met, without any equivalent responsibilities being
imposed on the beneficiary. In the political sense, the modern
adult is therefore radically unin-formed.

The physically mature being who emerges from this unneces-
sarily prolonged chrysaline state of nonreciprocal dependence now
enters another world in which some element of reciprocity between citizen and state is inevitable, however unprepared for it the
individual may be. The institutions of modern society, attuned as

they are primarily to the servicing of private aspiration, depend, like all institutions, on the involvement of the citizens who must maintain them in being. In the classical *polis*, this involvement was concrete and direct, taking the form of legislative, judicial, and military service within a polity that was experienced as both the precondition of survival and the vehicle of self-realization, which was achieved, above all, through such service. In the modern state, involvement is abstract and mediated primarily through the giving and taking of money. For the majority of citizens, the most striking sign of their inescapable involvement with the public sphere is not the vote they cast in an election every four or five years, but the monetary bond represented, on the one hand, by the payment of taxes and, on the other, by the drawing of financial benefits.

The form of reciprocity in this form of political involvement is not merely abstract but potentially socially divisive. The taxpayer perceives his payments as serving, in large part, the private aspirations of other individuals for whose well-being he has little sense of responsibility. The beneficiary takes his benefits for granted and so fails to grasp the political ethic of reciprocal responsibility and service essentially involved in every institutional order. An element of mutual resentment grows up between the two, and if the division of the citizenry into two mutually exclusive classes of givers and takers corresponded to the true situation the effect would, in view of the primacy accorded to individual desires, produce a state of chronic class hostility that might destroy civil society. In fact, however, most citizens are both givers and takers, taxpayers and beneficiaries; and so resentment, while being mollified, is displaced from the relationship between citizens to that between the citizen and the state. Social divisiveness is moderated, but at the cost of further alienating man from the imperatives of his political condition.

This can be illustrated by the way in which expenditure on national defense, which remains the precondition for the preservation of a relatively autonomous private sphere within an independent political whole, is popularly regarded, especially in Western Europe, as somehow less valuable than the provision of noncondi-tional benefits in education and welfare. The appeal exerted by the so-called Peace Movement, whose typically unilateralist nonreciprocal approach to questions of defense reveals a sublime contempt for the realities of political survival, is symptomatic of a wider decline in political in-formation among the peoples of the West. In liberal-democratic societies, the publicly financed activities of the state, while always resented, are most readily tolerated when they most directly serve what have become the morally preeminent aspirations of private existence. Since the benefit of effective defenses is, except in times of war, knowable in only an indirect and negative sense, there is always pressure to transfer resources from this most fundamental of authentically public responsibilities to others whose effects are felt more immediately in private life. The statesman who, in such a society, remains aware of the true order of political imperatives always faces an uphill struggle in his efforts to maintain the means of effective defense in a cultural environment in which such necessities seem abstract, remote, and even morally repulsive. The ability of the Peace Movement to attract support from outside traditionally pacifist circles and beyond the range of Soviet sympathizers is one of the most striking signs of the eclipse of reality among people who no longer understand the political factors that make their privileged existences possible. As such, it is symptomatic of a malaise that threatens us all.

Mine has been a work of analysis and exploration. I have, I believe, outlined a number of problems that are anchored in the unchanging constitutive conditions of human existence but have, in the modern world, reached an acute stage. Anyone who accepts the outlines of this analysis will, I assume, take comfort from the fact that there are still a number of political leaders who accept its practical implications and continue to guide public policy in ways that are, as I have argued, at variance with certain profound and dangerous tendencies in social and moral evolution. The use of the term *evolution* and the emphasis on the deep-seated nature of these trends should not hypnotize us into believing that there is any necessity about the outcome of future events. The future is open, and even the most pessimistic of diagnoses does not, in the sphere of human action, entail a fatal prognosis.

The problem of maintaining a balance between man and the world whose being he must now sustain is indeed a grave one. So is the problem of resisting ideologically motivated forces, which—

by rationalizing some of the most emotionally ingrained aspirations of a being who experiences the tension of finite freedom—exert a permanent disruptive pressure on political order. The secular horizon of modern man and, with it, the loss of the measure of Divine transcendence aggravate these problems enormously. And the fact that the revelatory experiences in which the transcendent measure of God's will is disclosed have, historically speaking, exerted most influence when the circumstances of worldly existence are most threatening, is only comforting to the extent that men understand the gravity of the present position. Modern technology, in isolating men, at least in the short term, from the consequences of their actions, creates an environment in which the realization of truth may come too late. But this too is mere possibility, and even a work of analysis, a theoretical gesture, may play a part in preventing it.

Indeed, in a world in which the conditions of life no longer produce a spontaneous acceptance of the political imperatives of human existence and fulfillment, it may be that only theoretical analysis can provide any sort of replacement at all. Let us admit that such a replacement is always inadequate. Proceeding by argument, its conclusions are always arguable and cannot form part of the taken-for-granted reality of the life-world in the way that the lessons implicit in the circumstances of agrarian existence once could. They will only exert any influence at all to the extent that they find a place in the general rhetoric of political persuasion. And that is the task, not of the theorist, but of the statesman.

INDEX

Culture (*continued*)
tion of, 85–86; Plessner's view of,
126–27

Dallmayr, Fred R., 125–26
Darwinian theory. *See* Evolution
De Maistre, Joseph, 48
Defense expenditures, 193–94
Descartes, René, 91
Determinism, 23, 66, 81
Dilthey, Wilhelm, 90
Divinity. *See* Spiritual life
Driesch, Hans, 66
Durkheim, Emile, 156–57

Ecology, 180, 181
Ecumenic Age, The (Voegelin), 106,
120–22
Eliade, Mircea, 12–13, 48, 102
Engels, Friedrich, 153
Epistemology, 125
Ethics, 141, 177
Ethics (Aristotle), 90
Ethik (Hartmann), 73
Ethology, 3, 28
Evolution, 2, 3, 18, 29–30, 67–69

Fatalism, 149–50
Fate, 149–50
Feeling, 4–5
Feminists, 165
Feuerbach, Ludwig, 150
Frazer, Sir James George, 12
Freedom: in animals, 8; human nature
and, 8, 19–20; finite nature of,
26–27, 39–41, 58–59, 84–85,
139–40; Hartmann's view of,
26–27, 39; causality and, 36; ontological, 39–40; political, 39; and instinct, 41; and institutions, 41;
Jonas' view of, 41–44, 126; versus
autonomy, 41; inorganic matter, 42,
44; living organism, 42–44; as
viewed by modern world, 139,
186–87

Gadamer, Hans-Georg, 47, 55, 166–68
Gebhardt, Jürgen, 94, 132
Gehlen, Arnold: Lorenz as critic of,
29; theory of institutions, 30, 42,
126, 190, 192; transformative action,

44–47; view of history, 46; view of
human nature, 50, 62–65, 66–67;
reformation of philosophical anthropology, 63, 65; critique of Hartmann, 65, 66; ontology in work of,
66; perfected biological approach,
66–67; review of organic philosophy, 66; comparison of human with
animal existence, 67–71; on evolution, 67–68; rejection of spirit, 67,
69; Scheler's influence on, 67, 80;
analogy with Gestalt psychology,
69–70; necessity of culture, 74, 75;
nature of human consciousness,
75–76; endorsement of sophistic
naturalism, 76; Landgrebe's critique
of, 76–78; affiliations with nineteenth-century positivism, 78; naturalism of, 114; view of Scheler, 114;
development of Voegelin's themes,
120; watersheds in history, 148;
agricultural economy, 155–56; Habermas' critique of institutionalism,
163–66; influence on Luckmann,
169; and problem of politics, 172;
secular horizon of man, 175
—works: *Der Mensch, seine Natur
and seine Stellung in der Welt*,
62–64, 66, 72, 73, 76, 81, 114
Genetics, 28, 41
Gestalt psychology, 69–70
Gnosticism, 107–12
God. *See* Religion; Spiritual life
Golden Bough, The (Frazer), 12
Greek philosophers: view of nature,
17; view of human nature, 72, 87,
109; political philosophy of, 84,
86–87, 164, 172–73, 182–86,
191–93; role of philosopher,
104–105, 106, 124; theory and practice of order, 104–105; view of reason, 104; nature of the soul, 135. *See
also* names of specific men

Habermas, Jürgen, 163, 183, 184, 186
Hartmann, Nicolai: on human nature,
2–3; meaning in the world, 10, 22;
prejudice in favor of simplicity, 12;
strata of real being, 18, 22–26,
29–30, 115, 130, 131, 133, 140;
structure of reality, 21; characteris-

028829

320.011 L4p 1987
Levy, David J.
Political order

028829

320.011 L4p 1987
Levy, David J.
Political order

DATE DUE	BORROWER'S NAME	ROOM NUMBER